designing a **book**

designing a **book**

derek brown

primrose hill press
bicester
2003

Published in Great Britain by Primrose Hill Press, Bicester, 2003.

Text and original illustrations © copyright Derek Brown 2003.

Designed by Derek Brown at Oblong Creative Ltd, Wetherby.

ISBN 1 901648 32 X casebound
ISBN 1 901648 33 8 paperback

British Library Cataloguing-in-Publication Data.

A catalogue record for this book is available
from the British Library.

9 8 7 6 5 4 3 2 1

PRINTED AND BOUND BY HENRY LING LTD, THE DORSET PRESS, DORCHESTER

contents

	introduction	7
1	how a book is made	10
2	materials	19
3	the parts of a book	25
4	format	34
5	layout	39
6	pictures	49
7	type and typography	62
8	equipment and method	98
9	note on editorial style	110
10	further reading	111
11	checklist	113
12	glossary	115
	index	127

introduction

ANYONE WITH A COMPUTER can make words appear on paper — and words on paper are all one needs to make a book. So, who needs to study book design?

Consider the person who, without the benefit of design training, keys pages on a computer and gives them to a printer. He or she has made several design decisions already: what typeface is to be used, what the page size is to be, what margins the page is to have, styles for the headings, spelling and punctuation conventions, the treatment of quotations and references, the form and number of preliminary pages, and more. The fact that they may have accepted the computer's defaults for most of these decisions does not absolve them of responsibility for them — it just means that the result will, in all probability, be a boring and ungainly book. In the absence of informed guidance, the printer in turn must make design decisions: what paper is to be used, how the book is to be bound, etc. Printers would much rather have a detailed specification — that way they can reasonably anticipate satisfaction and, so long as they follow the specification properly, they are not culpable if the book fails to please.

The wide availability of desktop-publishing software has led to a deluge of ineptly designed publications, many of which do not do justice to their content. I have tried in this book to offer a solution to that problem by giving guidance and a grounding in first principles to those who find that they must design a book without training or experience.

In addition, the designer coming belatedly to computers may find in these pages the new knowledge which I had quickly to acquire myself in order to function as a computer-aided designer/typesetter. It is a consequence of the involvement of computers in design that the skilled crafts of typesetter and compositor are usurped by the often less skilled designer.

Although the book is set out in such a way that it can be used as a reference manual, it is to be hoped that some readers will have the curiosity and perseverance to read it from cover to cover.

HAVING IDEAS

It is a fallacy to imagine that all good ideas in design are entirely original. Every design owes a debt to others that have gone before it. There would be no development or discernible history of design if it were not so. This is to say not that the new is always an improvement on the old, but that a design which does not acknowledge the influences of past and present may not be as successful as a design which does.

So, it is necessary to make a distinction between leaving yourself open to the influence and inspiration of the work of other designers and uncritically copying designs which appeal to you. When looking at such a model, three questions to ask yourself are 'Do I know why I like this design?', 'Do I understand how this design works?', and 'Do I have the right problem for this solution?' (because design, as any designer will tell you, is about solving problems). If the answer to all three questions is 'Yes', then there is something to be learned from the design in question. Your understanding of how the design works will help you to distil the relevant elements from it. Look at the grid structure, the typeface, the size and spacing of the type, the treatment of illustrations, the use of colour, the materials used … and decide which, if any, have relevance for your work. Keep examples of design which excites you and use them as inspiration.

To broaden the process a little further, seek out other visual, and even non-visual, influences: art books and galleries, architecture, engineering, and music, for instance, all contain themes and ideas which find an echo in typography and book design.

FITNESS FOR PURPOSE

With the inspiration of the design environment you have created for yourself, and with the help of this book, you should be able to take a creditable stab at any book-design problem which confronts you. The final test of your solution might be whether or not your employer or client likes it or, if it is a commercial publication, whether people buy it: but there is another, more fundamental measure of success which you should apply to your ideas at every stage of the process — fitness for purpose.

When I was attending art college in the late 1960s, design education in Britain still benefited from the influence of European designers who had fled the Nazis in the 1930s and 40s.

They were respectfully referred to as 'Bauhaus refugees' and, although they were not all directly associated with it, they brought with them the design philosophy for which the Bauhaus is best remembered — put simply, the more functional an object is, the more beautiful it ought to be. Today, we have lived through a 'post-modernist' age and must acknowledge other criteria, but common sense tells us that the converse implication of Bauhaus theory, that if a thing does not fulfil its function it should not be said to be 'beautiful', still applies.

Before you embark on the problem-solving exercise of design, think about the functional requirements of the book you are about to shape and consider the options available to you to make it fit for its purpose.

ACKNOWLEDGEMENTS

In the course of writing this book I have had cause to be grateful to the following: my father, Richard Brown, for first interesting me in lettering; Stan Maney, with whose knowledge of type and its history I could not compete; Dr Brian Hill and Rose Siviter for their forbearance and advice; Professor Bill Butler, my publisher, for his enthusiasm; Ken Smith for checking sections on binding; my friends Liz and Geoff Darlington, for tip-toeing around me and my laptop in a holiday cottage in Burgundy; Jackie Maidment of Oblong for reading the first proofs, and Karen, my wife, for her encouragement and for reading everything as it was written.

I would also like to express my gratitude to Primrose Hill Press, Maney Publications, Smith Settle, The Society of Architectural Historians of Great Britain, and The Chapels Society for permission to reproduce pages from their publications.

DEREK BROWN

1 how a book is made

1.1 INTRODUCTION

Until the second half of the twentieth century most typesetting, book printing, and binding was done by methods which would readily have been understood by Gütenberg or Caxton. Even the pre-computer mechanization of typesetting, though a wonder of engineering, would have been comprehensible to any printer with a grasp of mechanics and mathematics.

Starting in the early years of the twentieth century but gaining ascendancy only in the 1970s, when it was combined with filmsetting, *offset lithography* revolutionized the making of books. In the 1980s and '90s, personal computers slotted themselves naturally into the process and sealed the fate of the old technology.

Metal type and *letterpress* printing still survive in various places around the world and continue to serve the special needs of some publishers and designers. New digital printing systems, which harness personal computers to digital copying technology to replace both film and lithographic printing, are an interesting development which has already had an impact on short-run printing and created a new market for 'on demand' books. However, at the start of the twenty-first century, imagesetting and offset lithography, together with binding methods which remain essentially traditional, are the means whereby most books are produced.

For the purposes of this book, then, we will concentrate on *scanning*, *imagesetting*, *offset lithography*, and *sewn* and *'perfect' binding*, since these are the processes which most book designers will encounter.

1.2 SCANNING

The pros and cons of designing with low-resolution scans (*positionals*) or reproduction-standard scans are discussed in

Metal type can be printed from at the same time as wood engravers' blocks on traditional printing presses.

The origination and layout of text, which once was the compositor's job, is now part of the design process and is discussed in 5 and 7. See also 8.7 and 9.

section 6.2. In gaining an understanding of the production process, we are concerned with the high-resolution scans required for printing. These are normally produced on a scanner belonging to a repro company or printer and result in an image file (see 6.4) which will ultimately form part of the page file from which the imagesetter produces film, or the platesetter — plates. The optimum quality obtainable from desktop scanners, particularly for tone work, is not usually good enough for reproduction and they are not discussed in this section.

In order to do his job, the scanner operator must know from the designer: the intended size of the image (expressed as a percentage), any large areas at the edges of the image to be 'masked off', whether the image is to appear as a monochrome (usually black-and-white) or colour picture, and — if monochrome — whether line or halftone reproduction is envisaged (see 6.3).

There may also be special requirements, such as the need to adjust the colour, 'drop out' the background or blur the edges of the image to create a 'vignette' effect.

1.3 IMAGESETTERS

The word *imagesetter* reflects the machine's function as an output device for pictures as well as text. If, as a designer, you are using desktop-publishing (*dtp*) software and working with reproduction-quality scans, the files which you produce will be *imposed* (see 1.5.1) by the printer and output as film. Output devices are of various sizes, affecting the number of pages which can be fitted on one piece of film and requiring, in the case of a small imagesetter and large printing format, hand assembly of two or more pieces of film before each printing plate is made. The process of film assembly is facilitated on some imagesetters by the automatic punching of the film with holes which exactly fit pins fixed on the assembly frame.

1.3.1 Platesetters

Computer-to-plate (*ctp*) technology is replacing imagesetting in some parts of the printing industry, including book printing. The machine which produces imposed printing plates from desktop-publisher files is called a *platesetter*. In most respects, it does not matter to the designer whether ctp or film is being used, except in the respect that proofing methods which require film (see 8.7.5) will not be used. In theory, ctp should result in a more perfect printed image, since it involves one less stage at which degradation can occur.

1.3.2 Colour

For colour printing, four pieces of film are produced by an imagesetter, or four plates by a platesetter, one for each of the four colours which go to make up a colour image. (See 1.4.1 for a description of colour printing.)

1.4 PRINTING

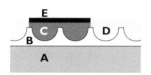

Schematic cross-section of a printing plate (greatly magnified) before exposure to light: A = aluminium plate; B = zinc coating; C = light-sensitive resin.

The film from the imagesetter is used to produce lithographic plates by means of a photochemical process. Film can be either negative or positive. Plates with different chemical coatings are exposed to light passing through the two types of film. In the case of negative film, the light hardens a resinous chemical. In the case of positive film, the effect of the light is to soften the chemical, which remains hard where unexposed. The subsequent processing of either kind of plate washes away the softer coating leaving an ink-receptive image. The end result of both processes is the same. The choice of negative or positive film may depend upon the printer's manual film-assembly requirements, or on the particular plate-processing equipment used by the printer. If, as a designer, you are dealing separately with a repro house and a printer, it is important that you discover the type of film required by the printer and instruct the repro company accordingly.

Printing plates can be made of a number of materials but the ones in general use for book printing are of aluminium coated with zinc, which is minutely pitted to make it receptive to water. As we have seen, the text and images, which are clearly legible on the plate's surface, are composed of an ink-receptive resin.

Cross-section of a printing plate at the point of printing: A = aluminium plate; B = zinc coating; C = resin; D = water; E = ink.

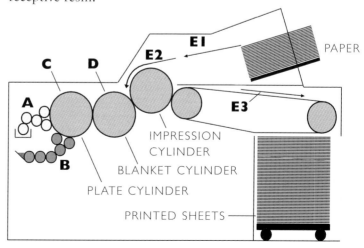

A sheet-fed offset-lithographic printing machine shown schematically: A = damper rollers; B = inking rollers; C = plate; D = rubber blanket; E1–3 = paper at three stages of its progress through the machine.

PAPER

IMPRESSION CYLINDER

BLANKET CYLINDER

PLATE CYLINDER

PRINTED SHEETS

The plate is bent around the surface of a large cylinder on the printing machine. The machine first wets the surface of the plate, then inks the image as the cylinder turns to bring it into contact with damper and inking rollers, then transfers the image onto a rubber blanket which is wrapped round another cylinder. On a *sheet-fed* printing press, a third cylinder grips the paper at one edge and brings it into contact with the rubber blanket, at which point the ink is transferred to the paper. The printed sheet is then released by the printing cylinder and stacked on top of those already printed.

Factors which can affect the quality of the printed image include:

- the amount of ink used. (Under-inking will result in grey type and 'flat' images. Over-inking or too little damping can produce fuzzy edges to type and line images, dark half-tone images with lost detail in the shadows, and *set-off* — the transfer of ink from one sheet to the next after printing.)

- the evenness of inking. (The machine spreads the ink by moving the rollers from side to side as they turn but, if the ink is unevenly fed to the rollers, parts of the printed area will appear darker than others. Equally, a dark image taking up a large amount of ink as it comes into contact with the inking roller may cause text and images in its wake to be under-inked and appear lighter.)

- the condition of the printing machine. (A clean, well maintained machine is, for example, less likely to produce images and areas of solid colour with little white spots in them.)

- the properties of the paper used. (See 2.3.6 where the surface qualities of different types of paper are discussed.)

1.4.1 *Four-colour printing*

To print in colour on a single-colour press it is necessary to pass each side of each sheet of paper through the machine four times — once each for cyan, magenta, yellow, and black, the four colours which together give the impression of full-colour reproduction. A four-colour press prints all four colours at one pass through the machine. In effect, it is four self-contained printing machines bolted together.

The advantage of a four-colour press to the designer who is fortunate enough to be involved at the moment of printing is that inking levels can be adjusted with the end result in view. When several colours are printed on a single-colour machine the designer must rely upon *densitometer* readings (which show the density of a printed solid square of the colour in question) and the operator's experienced eye.

Some colour machines have more than four printing units — allowing extra colours to be used in addition to the four process colours or for varnish to be 'printed' on to specific parts of the image.

1.4.2 Spot colour

A fifth colour, in addition to the four process colours used for colour printing, or a second colour, in addition to black, may be needed. Such a colour is called a spot colour. A five-colour press can print an extra colour at the same pass as the other four. A four colour press requires an extra pass for a fifth colour and a single-colour press for a second colour. The ink for a spot colour is mixed specially and can be any colour. Spot colours are commonly specified using the *Pantone* colour-matching system.

1.4.3 Perfectors

If an ordinary printing press is used, each sheet must be passed through the machine two times so that both sides can be printed. *Perfectors* are machines which print both sides at one pass through.

1.4.4 Web offset printing

For longer runs, particularly when colour is needed, a *web* press may be used. Web machines work in the same way as sheet-fed machines but the paper is in the form of a reel which is fed continuously through the machine until it has come into contact with the blanket cylinder the requisite number of times. The reel is then cut into sheets — often as part of an automated binding line (see 1.5.9).

1.5 BINDING

There are many possible processes involved in binding a book — some of them hand operations which have not changed in essence since before the invention of printing from type. A designer with a generous budget or with unusual technical requirements would be well advised to discuss the range of possibilities with the binder. For the purposes of this book we will concentrate on the most common options: *sewn*, *perfect*, *paperback*, and *cased* binding.

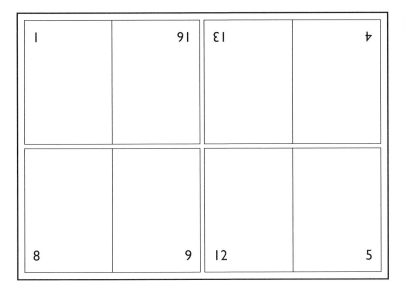

8-pages-to-view imposition — the outer side of a 16-page section

1.5.1 Imposition

Imposition is the arrangement of pages on the printed sheet so that, when folded by the binder, they will appear in the correct sequence.

There are standard impositions for 8-, 12-, 16-, and 32-page sections and there is rarely a need for the printer and binder to consult each other about these except, perhaps, to agree the amount of *trim* to be left around the edges. However, if your design may involve folding the sheet unconventionally or pasting single leaves on to folded sections, it is important that you, the printer, and the binder discuss the imposition at the outset.

1.5.2 Folding

Once the imposition is agreed the folding of the sheets is a relatively straightforward mechanical process. Take care, however, that the weight of paper you have specified (see 2.3.1) is not too great or too little to be successfully folded on the folding machine.

1.5.3 Collating and gathering

After the sections have been folded they are collated. This may involve insetting sections into the centre of others to make larger sections or simply gathering the sections side-by-side in the right order. This process can be automated but, for short to medium runs, it is usually a manual operation. Pasting (or *tipping*) single sheets or foldouts (folded leaves, such as maps,

Fold any sheet of paper in half three times — each time at right angles to the last — and you will have a model of an untrimmed sixteen-page *binding section* (or *signature*). Hold it with the visible corners of the original sheet at the bottom right, number the pages consecutively with a pen without tearing them, and open the sheet flat: you will see the imposition for one side of an *eight-pages-to-view* sheet. Turn it over and you have the *imposition* for the other side.

Take a book and flick through the pages, focusing on the *folios* (page numbers). If they appear to jump up and down, this is most likely the result of poor folding.

which unfold to a larger size than the trimmed page) on to the sections takes place before gathering.

1.5.4 Sewing and stitching

If the book is not to be 'perfect' bound (see 1.5.6) it must be sewn or wire-stitched. Wire-stitching holds the book (which must be one section only — usually of no more than 64 pages) together by means of stitches (staples) through its centre and is more appropriate for booklets than for most books.

The workings of a sewing machine could be said to defy analysis by the layman (as do those of the domestic sewing machine). Fortunately, it is enough to know that threads are passed through the centre of each folded section and between each section and its neighbours in such a way that when the top, front, and bottom edges are trimmed off the book it does not fall apart.

Before it is covered or trimmed the sewn book is called a *book block* or *sewn middle*. The advantages of sewing over 'perfect' binding are the greater facility with which the book can be opened flat and less of a tendency for the book to become weakened and fall apart after repeated opening. It is generally regarded as the stronger form of binding.

1.5.5 Endpapers

If a sewn book is to be cased, rather than paper bound, it will usually have endpapers. These are the folded four-page sheets of paper (often a different paper from that of the book's pages) which are attached to the inside of the binding case and form the first and last leaves of the book. Endpapers are sometimes attached to the first and last sections before sewing and sometimes to the sewn middles after sewing. The design of the book may call for endpapers which are printed and/or of coloured paper. The term 'self-ends' refers to the less than satisfactory option of using the first and last pages of the sewn book as endpapers. Endpapers are not given page numbers.

1.5.6 Perfect binding

An alternative to sewing, usually associated with paper covers, is *perfect binding*. This entails cutting the backs off gathered sections and gluing them directly to the inside of the cover. The back of the gathering (or *book block*) is roughened to ensure good adhesion, and different means of doing this have occasionally given rise to attempts to re-name the process. None of these proprietary names has achieved wide currency.

Perfect binding is quicker and cheaper than sewing and can more easily be incorporated into an automated binding line. It is used for mass-market paperbacks, for books with very few pages, and occasionally because the designer or publisher prefers to sacrifice the superior strength and functionality of sewn binding for the neater, sharper edges which perfect binding can give to the book's spine.

1.5.7 Case binding

The term refers to the case of rigid board (usually *grey board*) with a flexible spine in which the book is bound. The boards themselves can be covered on the outside with a range of materials including printed paper, embossed paper cloth substitutes, cloth of various kinds, plastics, and leather. These materials can be *blocked* with metallic or non-metallic foils (see, for example, the lettering on the spine of most cased books), *blind blocked* (which gives a depressed design without foil), or scored, raised, shaped, printed, etc. by a number of traditional methods. Additionally, the spine can be flat or rounded (the term 'rounded and backed' is used to describe the preparation of the sewn middle and the resultant shape of the spine). The design possibilities inherent in cased binding are often overlooked and much can be said for creative collaboration between designer and binder before the binding specification is fixed.

1.5.8 Paperback binding

The above description of 'perfect' binding touches on the covering process. In 'perfect' binding, a flat printed cover of board (heavier than the paper of the pages but much lighter than the boards used for case binding) is glued and shaped around the back of the pages so that the glue both holds the pages together and sticks the cover to the pages.

Such a cover is often called a *drawn-on* cover. For shorter runs or for greater strength and openability it is also common to bind *sewn* middles in a drawn-on cover. The process is the same as for perfect binding except that the sewing holds the pages together so that the glue is only required to hold the cover to the sewn middle.

Books with drawn-on covers (paperbacks) are trimmed to size after they are covered. Case-bound books are trimmed after they are endpapered but before they are cased.

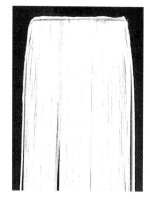

A perfect-bound, paperback book

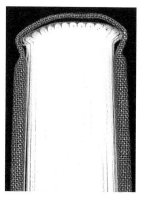

A case-bound, sewn book

1.5.9 Automation

It may be evident from the above descriptions that book binding can be a matter of several separate operations, some of them manual, or of one automated 'line'. Automated binding lines take up the printed sheets or reels from a printing machine at one end and deliver trimmed paperbacks at the other. They are usually associated with long runs. Short-run binding commonly involves a lot more human intervention. What constitutes a short run and what a long one, however, is a matter of your point of view. Ten thousand books is a long run to a short-run binder but would be regarded as a short run by a printer of popular paperbacks.

2 materials

2.1 INTRODUCTION

Changes in the types of paper available to the book designer tend to be driven by the advertising and packaging industries rather than by book publishing, which accounts for a relatively small part of the market. So, it can be a frustrating search if you are looking for off-white or cream, uncoated paper with a smooth surface, high opacity, and archival properties in a size which suits your book — especially so if you are proposing to use a quantity of less than two *tonnes*.

2.2 PAPER

Papers fall into a number of categories and have properties which define them and indicate their suitability for different kinds of book.

When I first worked in publishing there were *book woves*, *laids*, *cartridges*, *coated cartridges*, and *art papers*. Today, the emphasis has shifted firmly towards the coated papers, which are now divided into more categories, and away from uncoated papers, which most paper merchants group together. The current list of paper types would include: *matt art*, *silk* or *satin*, *gloss art*, and *tinted* papers, as well as speciality papers, many of which are tinted and embossed. In an age in which conservation and ecology are gaining ground, there is also a growing number of acid-free, chlorine-free, and/or recycled papers, some of which are excellent book papers.

2.2.1 Coated and art papers

The coating on these papers contains china clay, which fills the space between the fibres that form the paper's natural surface and renders it smooth. Today, it is difficult to identify any difference between art papers and other kinds of coated paper. Matt art papers have taken over from coated cartridges; gloss art papers continue to provide a good surface for difficult *half-tone* images; and silk or satin coated papers provide the best of both worlds. In fact, all coated papers give good results when half-tones are printed on them by lithography (but beware of the tendency for the surface of some matt and silk varieties to 'rub' or crack when bound). Many designers prefer the non-reflective, more tactile surface of matt and silk papers to the impenetrable sheen of true (gloss) art papers.

There is a regrettable quest amongst paper manufacturers to make their coated papers ever whiter, and thus ever harder on the reader's eye.

2.2.2 Offsets and cartridges

Offsets are uncoated cartridge papers below a certain weight (see 2.3.1). In general, above 90 grams per square metre (*gsm*) the paper is a cartridge, and below that weight it is an offset. Although uncoated, the smooth surface of most cartridges and offsets makes them suitable for picture printing of a general kind. They come in white and tinted varieties, the white being prone to yellowing after prolonged exposure to light, and are readily available in ISO sizes (see 4.4). The yellowing stems partly from the use of bleach in their manufacture. There are, however, some cartridges on the market which have neutral acidity and are bleach-free. Such papers have a natural off-white or ivory colour and are near archival in their longevity, as well as being ecologically sound, but are hard to come by in small quantities because there is insufficient demand for them.

2.2.3 Woves

The word 'wove' refers to the fine wire mesh of the tray in which the paper used to be made in earlier times and which gave it a smoother surface than that of *laid* paper. Book woves (as distinct from wove stationery papers, which concern us less) have an open texture wherein the fibres can easily be seen with a magnifying glass or felt with the tip of a finger. They tend to be of a pleasing, cream colour, and are usually long-lasting, being close to neutral acidity and relatively free from bleach. Their comparatively rough, absorbent surface makes them inappropriate for much illustrated work (although they are fine for simple *line* images). The rougher and less compressed they are, the more opaque they ought to be — since the amount of air within the paper makes them so. There has over the years been a decline in opacity of book woves.

Because they are of little interest to commercial printers, book woves are often unobtainable in less than *making quantities* (see 2.3.1). Many of them are manufactured in the old Imperial sizes.

2.2.4 Laid papers

Laid papers have a texture of parallel lines, closely spaced in one direction (perpendicular to the *grain*, see 2.3.2) and widely spaced in the other (parallel to the grain). This impression was once made by the coarse wire mesh on which the paper pulp lay as the water drained from it, but today it is usually created artificially by embossing the paper after manufacture. Laid papers are associated with stationery in the minds of most people but some are sold for general and book printing.

2.2.5 Speciality papers

There are many papers which fall outside the above categories. Among them are hand- and mould-made papers, which are still made by traditional craft processes and are consequently very expensive; embossed and tinted papers, which have uses in advertising and stationery but can also be used for covers, dust-jackets, and endpapers; and even more unusual materials such as plastic paper-substitutes.

2.2.6 Boards

Boards, used in book printing for covers, may be heavy-weight versions of papers (see 2.3.1). Matt-coated and art boards fall into this category — below 175 *gsm* they are called papers, above 200 *gsm* they are boards. Other boards have no paper-weight equivalent.

As with paper, some imaginatively tinted, textured, and embossed boards are available to the designer.

In *case binding*, very thick boards, such as *grey board* and *mill board*, are used. These are long-lasting, resilient materials and are usually specified by thickness (microns or millimetres) rather than weight (see 2.3.1). Mill board is a very dense board which is used less than grey board because it is more expensive: specify it if strength is the prime consideration and money is no object.

2.3 PROPERTIES OF PAPER

2.3.1 Weight

The weight of paper is expressed, in Europe, in grams per square metre, abbreviated to *gsm*. The more compressed a paper is, the heavier it needs to be to provide adequate *bulk* and *opacity*. So, coated papers between 100 gsm and 175 gsm are most suitable for book printing, as are offsets and cartridges between 90 gsm and 150 gsm and woves between 80 gsm and 100 gsm. These are merely guidelines — papers within these categories vary greatly in quality and appearance and weights outside these parameters may often prove suitable.

A *tonne* equals .9842 *tons*

Paper is priced either by weight or number of sheets. In Europe the unit of weight for pricing purposes is the tonne. The quantity to which prices refer is usually one thousand sheets, although for heavy weights, especially boards, the price of one hundred sheets is often given. Papers which are not stocked by merchants are normally available only in *making quantities*, which may be anything from 2 to 7 tonnes minimum.

Paper merchants' catalogues usually give the kilograms per thousand sheets. This factor allows the numerate designer to convert price per tonne to price per thousand sheets. The relevant equations are as follows:

Where sheet dimensions in millimetres = a x b
and paper weight in grams per square metre = g

$$\frac{a \times b \times g}{1,000,000} = \text{kilograms per thousand sheets}$$

Where kilograms per thousand sheets = k

$$\frac{1,000,000}{k} = \text{sheets per tonne}$$

Where sheets per tonne = s
and price per tonne = p

$$\frac{1000 \times p}{s} = \text{price per thousand sheets}$$

2.3.2 Grain direction

Paper is made of fibres which tend to lie in one direction. The direction in which most of the fibres lie is called the grain direction. Paper folds most easily parallel to the grain and is least likely to stretch at right angles to the grain. (See 4.6.)

2.3.3 Opacity

You can compare the opacity of two papers for yourself by laying them side-by-side over a printed page, or you can ask the paper supplier to provide comparative information. Several of the national and international merchants have laboratories where they can test all of a paper's qualities for you.

Opacity is an important property to consider when choosing a paper for book printing. An otherwise well-designed book can lose a lot of its impact if the reader has to put up with text and images showing through from the other side of the page or from the page following. Paper opacity is one of the subtle indicators which distinguish a shoddy book from one worth cherishing, yet it is not customary for paper merchants' catalogues to volunteer opacity statistics. The most common measurement of opacity is the percentage of light which is reflected by the paper's surface — a high value on a scale of 0–100 indicating high opacity.

2.3.4 Thickness (or calliper)

Usually expressed in microns (thousandths of a millimetre), the thickness of a given weight varies enormously between paper types. An 80 gsm book wove will usually be thicker than a 115 gsm matt art paper. Some publishers like a book to be as bulky as possible (in the belief that readers buy books by volume). High bulking book woves generally have good opacity and are available in off-white and cream shades.

Thickness is reduced by *calendering* (passing the paper between rollers as part of the paper-making process) or *super calendering* (rolling the paper in the same way after it has been made). (See 2.3.6 below.)

2.3.5 Acidity and alkalinity

Acidity causes paper to become brittle and discoloured. The measurement of acidity/alkalinity is the paper's pH value. A value under 7 is acidic — over 7 is alkaline. There are standards of longevity set by the Library of Congress. Paper which meets these standards (which require the paper to keep its original qualities for 300 years) are often over-priced, but pH neutral papers (which possess almost the same archival properties) are easily obtainable and may be reasonably priced.

2.3.6 Smoothness and surface

The smoothest of papers is gloss art paper, the surface of which is made of china clay, calcium carbonate, starch, and latex. Very fine line work and high-resolution halftone printing can be done most successfully on gloss art paper. Matt art papers offer almost as good a surface without the reflectivity of gloss, which tends to come between the reader and the subject — a little like placing artefacts in glass cases. Matt art papers are used today for a wide range of applications. Apart from coated papers, the smoothest papers are those which have been calendered or super-calendered (see 2.3.4). Most kinds of image can be printed with a measure of success on smooth, uncoated papers. Ordinary cartridge papers and book woves can successfully be used for text and coarse line images, and can be attractive and easy on the eye. The roughest of paper surfaces are found on hand- and mould-made papers. These are specialist papers which, because they are expensive, are used mainly for limited editions. Their surface texture is perceived as being one of their positive qualities. As with other comparatively rough papers, they do not lend themselves to fine halftone printing. However, there are occasions when definition might justifiably be sacrificed in favour of other desirable effects such as that produced by printing colour images onto a textured surface.

2.3.7 Tints and shades

Some papers owe their colour to the degree to which they are, or are not, bleached. Others, *tinted* papers, are coloured by means of pigments added in the manufacturing process. Art papers are not normally available in any other colour than white, although some are made in cream and ivory shades. Uncoated tinted papers and boards, especially the more up-market ones, are useful to the book designer as covers and endpapers. The creams, buffs, and greys can also make good text papers in appropriate circumstances. However, there is a depth and consistency to naturally cream paper which is not matched by tinted papers.

2.4 OTHER MATERIALS USED IN BOOK PRODUCTION

2.4.1 Binding materials

There is a wide range of materials used in cased bookbinding. Apart from cloths and imitation cloths (really embossed papers), there are leathers and plastics. As well as their different visual effects, these materials have various properties — making them suitable for different types of book. Waterproof and 'wipe-clean' products, for example, are particularly appropriate for handbooks used in industry or the home. The cost of binding materials varies dramatically and should be investigated before a choice is made.

2.4.2 Plastic paper

Plastic 'paper' has been available for many years now, although it has not made any noticeable impact on the sale of conventional papers. The chief virtue of plastic paper is that it is almost impossible to tear. It also has the advantage of being waterproof and I have seen one example of an instructional book printed on plastic because it had to be read by divers under water.

3 the parts of a book

3.1 INTRODUCTION

Between its covers, a book has several parts — few of them obligatory, but most of them occupying a recognized place in the order of appearance. In brief, and typically, they are:

Half-title

Frontispiece

Title page

Title verso

Dedication

Contents list

List of illustrations

Foreword

Author's preface

Acknowledgements

List of abbreviations

Introduction

Text

Appendix (or appendices)

Notes and references

Bibliography

Index (or indexes).

3.2 HALF-TITLE

Originally intended to keep the title page clean as the book awaited binding on a bookseller's shelf, the half-title provides a fixing place for cover or endpapers, allowing the title page to be opened flat. It is also a convenient location for series information (if the book is one in a series), a list of other books by the same author, or a brief biography of the author. There are

other peripheral bits and pieces which publishers choose to put on half-titles. It is regarded as an optional page today but, before deciding to dispense with it, consider its potential usefulness.

The *verso* (reverse side) of the half-title is traditionally left blank. Again it can be used for odd items like other books in the same series or books by the same author or, since offset lithography has made possible the printing of high-quality illustrations on text paper, a frontispiece. It can also become the left-hand half of a title *spread* in place of a title page.

Half-title

The Contexting of a Chapel Architect: James Cubitt 1836–1912, The Chapels Society, 2001

3.3 FRONTISPIECE

A frontispiece is an illustration which faces the title page. It always used to be, and often still is, printed on glossy art paper and pasted (*tipped*) onto the half-title verso. It provides an extra flourish, emphasizing the formal function of the title page. These days, it makes sense to print the frontispiece on the half-title verso (providing that the text paper is suitable), saving the considerable expense of the handwork involved in attaching a separate page.

When designing a frontispiece, remember that it is part of a double-page spread and should possess a definite and deliberate spatial relationship with the type on the title page.

A frontispiece and title page bearing a definite and deliberate spatial relationship

An Engraver's Globe, 2002

3.4 TITLE PAGE

The title page should contain the title of the book (and subtitle if there is one), the name of the author, the name of the publisher, and may also give the place and date of publication. The author of another work, wishing to cite the book in a reference, should be able to find on the title page everything he or she needs to know.

From the designer's point of view, it is preferable that the title page should contain no more than this. It is an opportunity for designers to use their skill to set the tone for the rest of the book.

You may have the chance to use an illustration on the title page, and for some books this is entirely appropriate, but more often than not it is with type alone that you must welcome and inform the reader. This is both a challenge and an opportunity, and it is instructive to take a few books off the shelf and see how other designers have approached it. The title page is always a *recto* (right-hand page) — usually page 3 or iii — but, where there is no frontispiece, it may extend onto the facing page, forming a title spread.

In general, the less clutter you have on a title page, the more effective it will be. Try to persuade publishers and authors that there are more appropriate places for dedications and epigraphs, and that the author's name on a title page need not be embellished with titles and qualifications.

A simple typographic title page

The Contexting of a Chapel Architect: James Cubitt 1836–1912, The Chapels Society, 2001

For more help on the typography of title pages and display typography in general, see 7.16 and 7.16.3.

3.5 TITLE VERSO

The reverse side (*verso*) of the title page contains the technical and bibliographical information which all books should carry. In its simplest form, it states the year of publication, the name of the copyright holder, the name of the publisher, and the International Standard Book Number (ISBN). It may also (and ought to) contain: the publisher's address; a copyright statement listing media (print, CD-Rom, etc.) by means of which it would be illegal to reproduce of any part of the work without permission of the copyright holder; British Library (in the USA, Library of Congress) Cataloguing in Publication (CIP) details, information about the typefaces and materials used, and the name and address of the designer, typesetter, printer, and binder. It used to be a legal requirement to name the printer because printers shared responsibility for libellous and defamatory statements made within the book. Happily this no longer applies but most printers, nevertheless, have a clause in their contract with publishers indemnifying them against such charges.

When designing the title page verso, try to group the type in the same position as type on the title page. This will avoid the type on the verso being visible through the paper (*show-through*) and spoiling the title page.

3.6 DEDICATION

An optional item requested by some authors, the dedication may occupy a page of its own, in which case it should fall *after* the title page, or it may have to be tucked away in a vacant space on one of the other preliminary pages (e.g., half-title, title verso, contents verso). It should not appear on the title page. The design of a dedication should not elevate it to the level of display. Set it in the centre of the page unless your design is emphatically asymmetric (see 5.6, 7.12, and 7.16), in the text size, possibly in italic, and to a narrower measure than the text.

3.7 CONTENTS LIST

Apart from the title page, the list of contents (usually starting on a *recto*) is the most important item in the prelims, and it should be approached with due attention to the reader's needs. It lists all the parts of the book that come after it. Look at the contents lists in books around you and try to ascertain what options are open to the designer. The two most important pieces of information to convey are what elements the book contains and on which page each starts. Of secondary importance, but usually necessary, is the relative status of the items listed. In some academic or multi-author books it is also helpful to make clear to the reader how long each item is.

It is conventional, and often desirable, to set a contents list to a narrower measure than normal text. This makes it easier to associate short chapter titles with their page numbers and causes the reader's eye to travel shorter distances to take in the information. The decision which seems to arouse most passion in discussion between publisher and designer is whether to place the page numbers at the ends of the chapter titles or to align them in a column at the right-hand limit of the measure: furthermore, if aligned in a column, whether leader dots are needed to show to which item each number belongs. Aligning

Contents list

The Contexting of a Chapel Architect: James Cubitt 1836–1912, The Chapels Society, 2001

page numbers at the right (*ranging them right*) is one of those puzzling conventions which are held dear by people who claim no other special knowledge of typography (see 7.16.3). The need for leader dots, or lines, to connect titles to their numbers is evidence of the unsuitability of this arrangement in many cases. On the other hand, grouping the numbers in a column makes it easy for the reader to assess the length of each chapter and may be appropriate where a sense of formality is sought — it may also provide structure and impact when a very short contents list is located in the middle of a large page.

Clarity is the essential feature of a successful contents list and sufficient space should be left between the items on the list for the reader easily to tell them apart. This sometimes means that the list occupies more than one page.

3.8 LIST OF ILLUSTRATIONS

Clearly redundant if there are no illustrations, and optional if there are, a list of illustrations may take its typographical lead from the design of the contents list. If there are a great many illustrations, there is an argument for making the type smaller than that of the contents list and grouping the lines more closely, but we are still working within the part of the book which a reader may consult before deciding to read the book and may frequently visit in the course of reading, so clarity and visual appeal are of equal importance.

3.9 FOREWORD

The foreword, by someone other than the author, normally takes the design of any other text item in the book, such as the introduction or a chapter. If there are no such models, as might be the case in a book of illustrations with very little text, invent one which gives it modest prominence, possibly treating its title in the same style as that of the contents list, and use it for any other peripheral sections of text which follow (acknowledge-ments etc.). If space and budget allow, it should start on a right-hand page (*recto*).

3.10 AUTHOR'S PREFACE

Like the foreword, the preface is an item which usually takes the design of the other text in the book. If possible, start on a new recto.

3.11 ACKNOWLEDGEMENTS

Acknowledgements may be treated as a separate item with status equal to that of the preface or it may follow it as a sub-section with a subheading. Politics or the nature of the text itself (e.g. 'Finally, I would like to acknowledge …') may decide this. An alternative, but less desirable, position for an acknowledgements page is at the end of the book, following the last chapter.

3.12 LIST OF ABBREVIATIONS

Not a feature of every book but an essential one in many academic works, a list of abbreviations should appear before the parts of the book which may contain the abbreviations listed. So it is better placed in the prelims than at the end of the book. Its design should emphasize clarity, with plenty of space between the abbreviations listed and not too much between them and their definitions.

3.13 INTRODUCTION

The introduction to a book is, in all but title, one of its chapters. Its design should reflect this. A decision may have to be taken as to whether its page numbering links it to the preliminary pages or to the text (in other words: whether it has *roman* or *arabic folios* — see 3.19 below).

3.14 TEXT

See Sections 6 and 7 for help with text and pictures and 4 and 5 for format and layout.

I have called the body of the book *text* but, of course, it may be heavily illustrated with very little text. It always makes sense to me to tackle the body of the book first then come back to the *prelims* and *endmatter* (appendices, indexes, etc.).

3.15 APPENDICES

Appendices sometimes appear before notes and references and sometimes after. If the notes and references contain references to the appendices and are to be grouped together, they should always come after the appendices. The design of appendices will depend on their content, which could be text, lists, tables, or illustrations. It is usually considered reasonable to set appendices in a smaller size than the text, reflecting their non-central status.

3.16 NOTES AND REFERENCES

Notes and references are most frequently found in academic books and the placing of them depends on a number of considerations. The three customary places are: at the foot of the page (*footnotes*); at the ends of chapters; and at the end of the book (*endnotes*). In some books there is no distinction between notes and references, whereas in others there may be both footnotes and bibliographical references.

In general, a note should not be essential to the understanding of the text. Long, discursive notes often contain information which the author has added after the first draft of the work and could not be bothered to incorporate. As the designer, you may have to content yourself with privately noting how much harder some of us work than others, but you may be involved at an early enough stage to suggest improvements. Notes containing references to works quoted in the text should be so placed that they are easy to find but do not interfere with the reading of the text. This often means putting them at the end of the book, sometimes at the foot (or side) of the page on which the reference occurs, but rarely at the end of the chapter — a place which is not easily found.

The references in the text itself are usually *superior figures* and should, whenever possible, be placed *after* the nearest punctuation — ideally, at the end of the sentence. This is because a superior figure has a white space beneath it which disrupts reading of the sentence unless it coincides with a natural break. To place it before the punctuation would separate the punctuation from the word preceding it, which looks inelegant and unnatural.

Set notes and references in a small size, such as 8-point, with only as much interlinear space (*leading*) as legibility requires.

3.16.1 *Harvard, or author-date, system*

The Harvard system of references, which is employed in most scientific and many other academic works, requires that the author and date of the work referred to be quoted in parentheses at the relevant point in the text. The reader then refers to a bibliography for a full reference. It is both economic and specific in that it avoids repeated full references yet lacks the sloppiness and ambiguity of repeated use of 'ibid.' and 'op. cit.'.

3.17 BIBLIOGRAPHY

A bibliography lists works which are referred to in the text. Strictly speaking, it does not contain 'further reading' although, in practice, it may. The designer must decide how important a part of the book it is and treat it accordingly. In a reference or instructional book, such as this one, it may be as important as any other part of the book and merit a type-size which reflects this. In other cases, it may be of interest only to the bibliographer and may not even qualify for its own page. You will sometimes see bibliographies tucked away under the acknowledgements at the end of an author's preface.

With the Harvard, or author-date, style of referencing, the bibliography is an integral part of the referencing system and should be placed where it can easily be found at all times (see 3.16.1).

3.18 INDEX

An index is not a peripheral or optional part of a book — if there is one, it is likely to be necessary — yet it does not require continuous reading and can, therefore, be set in a small size. It is both economic and helpful to the reader to set indexes with short entries in double column. Clarity is the prime aim of the designer when approaching an index and this can be achieved by typographic simplicity, minimal punctuation (but not so minimal as to create ambiguity), moderate indentation, and measures such as dividing the index into letters of the alphabet by means of spaces, or employing bold and italic type to imply main references and illustrations.

3.19 PAGE NUMBERING

Conventionally, preliminary pages have their page numbers, or *folios*, as roman numerals (i, ii, iii, iv, etc.) and the main part of a book, and anything following it, has arabic figures (1, 2, 3, etc.). This may be useful in helping the reader to navigate, and it is specific with regard to what constitutes the book proper, but it gives rise to the question of when does the change occur — for example, is the introduction part of the prelims or of the book?

A commercial reason for not using roman numerals for preliminary pages is that it might mislead potential buyers as to how many pages they are getting for their money. A book numbered throughout in arabic numerals has a larger final page number than one with roman-numbered prelims. You and the publisher must decide how much you are swayed by this argument.

Regardless of the system of page numbering, several of the pages of a book carry no visible page number at all (although they are implicitly counted in). The half-title, half-title verso, title page, title page verso, dedication, first page of the contents list, first page of the list of illustrations, and first pages of acknowledgements and abbreviations do not normally carry a page number. The second and subsequent pages of the contents, list of illustrations, and other preliminary items usually do. Optional, and dependant primarily upon design considerations, are the folios at the foot of first pages of chapters. (If your design has folios at the heads of pages, they should never appear in that position on chapter-opening pages. Although there is a convention which allows you to place them at the foot — within or without the text area — it is more normal to omit them altogether on such pages.)

4 format

4.1 INTRODUCTION

The limits of page size have always been determined by the sizes in which paper is made and those of the machines used to print books. The rise of desktop publishing has helped ISO sizes, such as A4 and A5, which had already established themselves in office stationery, to eclipse traditional sizes. However, there are many occasions upon which traditional sizes offer the best solutions and a designer should feel free to adapt traditional and modern sizes, within the confines imposed by paper and printing machines, to suit the needs of the book.

4.2 PAGE FORMAT AND ECONOMY

The folded sections of a book (see 1.5.1–1.5.3) always consist of multiples of four pages and will usually be found to have 8, 12, 16, 24, or 32 pages. Some printing firms regularly print as few as four pages on one side of a sheet (resulting in an eight-page section) whilst others equipped with larger machines expect to print 16 or 32 pages 'to view'. In general, the larger the machine and the longer the run, the cheaper the book. On the other hand, smaller machines and shorter runs are sometimes associated with the highest quality of work.

If you are asked, as a designer, to decide the page size, try to discover the minimum and maximum practical sheet sizes for the printer's machines and choose a size which allows a viable arrangement of pages (see 1.5.1) to come out of an available size of the paper you propose to use (see 4.4 below).

4.3 TRIMS AND BLEEDS

To obtain a book with neat, openable pages, the binder trims a small margin from the head, *foredge*, and bottom of the book. The standard width of this margin is 3 mm and it should never be less. Your page size should allow for the fact that this 'trim' must come out of the sheet of paper to be used.

The trimming of books is not the most accurate of processes and, however much care is taken, there will always be a small difference between the page width at the centre of a section and that at the outside. For these reasons, a picture or area of tone which is supposed to extend to the edge of a page must, in reality, extend beyond it for at least 3 mm. This *bleed* will be more or less removed when the book is trimmed.

4.4 STANDARD SIZES

Traditionally, the system for naming page sizes in Britain depended on the number of times an 'Imperial' sheet size was folded to obtain them. Thus, a Crown sheet folded in half was called 'Crown Folio', in quarters 'Crown Quarto', and in eighths 'Crown Octavo'. In the 1960s several of the traditional sizes were 'metricized' and emerged as (amongst others) *Metric Crown* (384 x 504 mm), *Metric Demy* (444 x 564 mm), and *Metric Royal* (480 x 636 mm). Since most printing machines are larger than these sizes, book papers were, and some still are, made in sizes such as *Metric Quad Crown* (768 x 1008 mm), *Metric Double Crown* (504 x 768 mm), *Metric Quad Demy* (888 x 1128 mm), etc. Because they replaced the pre-metric Imperial sheets of the same names, the word 'Metric' was quickly dropped. The most popular trimmed book-page sizes derived from these sheets are *Crown Quarto* (246 x 189 mm), *Demy Octavo* (216 x 138 mm), and *Royal Octavo* (234 x 156 mm).

At the same time as the metricizing of Imperial paper sizes, the ISO 'A' and 'B' sizes came into use. These sizes, in particular A4 and A5, are known to most people in Europe, and much of the rest of the world, as stationery sizes and the sizes to which word-processor and desktop-publishing programs default. (In the USA there are different sizes which fulfil the same function. See marginal note.)

'A' sizes have a simple naming system. Their proportions of √2:1 mean that an 'A' size sheet cut in half parallel to its shorter side

The most commonly used ISO 'A' sizes

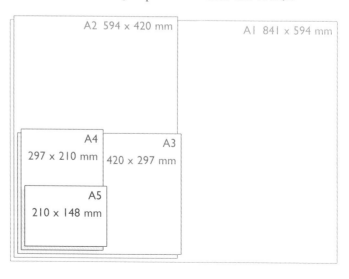

Crown Quarto
246 x 189 mm
(20% actual size)

245 x 175 mm
so-called 'B5'
(20% actual size)

Royal Octavo
234 x 156 mm
(20% actual size)

Demy Octavo
216 x 138 mm
(20% actual
size)

produces two sheets whose sides are in the same ratio as the original sheet. $A1$ (841 x 594 mm) cut in half is $A2$ (594 x 420 mm), $A2$ cut in half is $A3$ (420 x 297 mm), and so on. 'RA' and 'SRA' sizes were created to produce printing sheets which could be folded and trimmed to 'A' sizes: so, if you want to end up with eight $A4$ (297 x 210 mm) pages (four on each side of the sheet) and you have pictures which bleed (see 4.3), you will use an $SRA2$ (450 x 640 mm) sheet.

'B' sizes were originally conceived to provide intermediate sizes between 'A' sizes, but they have become standard maximum sheet sizes for many printing machines. Books, especially short-run ones, are often produced on $B1$ (720 x 1020 mm) or $B2$ (520 x 720 mm) sheet-fed machines. Note that the 'B' sizes do not quite conform to the halving or doubling principle which determines 'A' sizes.

4.5 AESTHETICS VERSUS ECONOMICS

It is clear that A4 and A5 pages make efficient use of widely available printing papers, and they are appropriate solutions for many book-design problems. However, many designers find them uninspiring or ill-suited to a range of tasks. For instance, A4 is too large for single-column text whilst A5 may be too small for certain types of illustrations. It is useful to remember that Crown Quarto (246 x 189 mm) provides an alternative to both. A popular, relatively new size, 245 x 175 mm, is close to Crown Quarto but fits 16-to-view on a $B1$ sheet. For this reason it is sometimes inaccurately termed 'B5'.

If you use desktop-publishing software, experiment with different standard page sizes. Try them with several text and image grids (see 5), fill the grids with a 30% tint of black for the images and/or body type for the text, print them out in double-page spreads, trim them to size and pin them to a wall. Stand back and try to decide what works well and what does not. You could also try adapting the standard sizes by shortening or narrowing them a little — A4 shortened by a few millimetres to, say, 280 x 210 mm is a popular variation. (If you are designing with pencil and paper you can, of course, do the same thing, but it will take you longer.)

Armed with this experience and, as time goes on, with the benefit of seeing your designs in print, you should be able to create a combination of format and layout which excites you, is appropriate to its task, and makes good use of the size of the printing machine.

4.6 GRAIN DIRECTION

The pages of a book open properly, and lie comparatively flat, if the grain direction is vertical (or, parallel to the bound edge of the pages). If a paper size is correctly expressed, the grain lies parallel to the last-named dimension. So, if the size is given as 450 x 640 mm (SRA2), the grain lies parallel to the long edge: the paper is a *long-grain* paper. Four A4 (297 x 210 mm) pages coming out of 450 x 640 mm will have the grain running in the right direction: eight A5 pages from the same sheet will not.

See 2.3.2.

It is only fair to say, however, that economic considerations often outweigh the arguments for correct grain direction, and that a book which refuses to lie open quite properly may be redeemed by other elements of its design.

4.7 PORTRAIT OR LANDSCAPE?

Unlike in paper sizes, where it denotes the grain direction, the order of the given dimensions of a *page* denotes its orientation. The first-mentioned dimension of a page is its vertical dimension. So '297 x 210 mm' describes a vertical, or *portrait*, page and '210 x 297 mm' describes a horizontal, or *landscape*, page.

It is worth noting that the authors of some desktop-publishing programs are unaware of this convention.

portrait

4.8 FORMAT, GRID, AND CONTENT

However much sense your format makes in terms of the paper sizes available to you, and however much you may like its proportions, it will not work if it is not appropriate for the content and layout requirements of the book you are designing. The next chapter discusses layout and should be referred to before you settle on a page format. Straightforward text, as encountered in a novel or biography, can be accommodated within a small format, such as A5 (210 x 148 mm) or Demy Octavo (216 x 138 mm), where a single column of text of readable length (see 7.11, 7.12) provides the most sensible solution. The presence of illustrations, particularly in large numbers, might lead you to favour a double-column layout, in which case you will need a larger page — e.g. Crown Quarto (246 x 189 mm), A4 (297 x 210 mm), or A4 landscape (210 x 297 mm). Otherwise the lines of text in your narrow columns will vary enormously in length or, if justified, contain some very large inter-word spaces. When experimenting with formats and

landscape

For discussion of type sizes and legibility, see 5.4, 7.10.3, 7.11.

grids (if you are using desktop publishing) try feeding text of sizes ranging from 9½ on 11 point to 12½ on 15 point into the text boxes and assessing it for readability.

However much sense your format makes in terms of the paper sizes available to you, and however much you may like its proportions, it will not work if it is not appropriate for the content and layout requirements of the book you are designing. The next chapter discusses layout and should be referred to before you settle on a page format. Straightforward text, as encountered in a novel or biography, can be accommodated within a small format, such as A5 (210 x 148 mm) or Demy Octavo (216 x 138 mm), where a single column of text of readable length (see 7.11, 7.12) provides the most sensible solution. The presence of illustrations, particularly in large numbers, might lead you to favour a double-column layout, in which case you will need a larger page — e.g. Crown

However much sense your format makes in terms of the paper sizes available to you, and however much you may like its proportions, it will not work if it is not appropriate for the content and layout requirements of the book you are design-ing. The next chapter discusses layout and should be referred to before you settle on a page format. Straightforward text, as encountered in a novel or biography, can be accommodated within a small format, such as A5 (210 x 148 mm) or Demy Octavo (216 x 138 mm), where a single column of text of readable length (see 7.11, 7.12) provides the most sensible solution. The presence of illustrations, particularly in large numbers, might lead you to favour a double-column layout, in which case you will need a larger page – e.g. Crown Quarto (246 x 189

However much sense your format makes in terms of the paper sizes available to you, and however much you may like its proportions, it will not work if it is not appropriate for the content and layout requirements of the book you are designing. The next chapter discusses layout and should be referred to before you settle on a page format. Straightforward text, as encountered in a novel or biography, can be accommodated within a small format, such as A5 (210 x 148 mm) or

However much sense your format makes in terms of the paper sizes available to you, and however much you may like its proportions, it will not work if it is not appropriate for the content and layout requirements of the book you are designing. The next chapter discusses layout and should be referred to before you settle on a page format. Straight-forward text, as encountered in a novel or biography, can be accommodated within a small format, such as A5 (210 x 148 mm) or Demy Octavo (216 x

---

Text set in narrow-column format in 9½ on 11 point (left) and 11½ on 15 point (right), unjustified (top) and justified (bottom). Clearly, such a column width does not work well for extended reading of sizes larger than 11 point. If the greater legibility of the larger size were to be preferred, a single-column layout on the same page size would be more successful. Alternatively, a double-column grid on a bigger page would work. In the right-hand examples the unjustified text at the top is easier on the eye than the justified text below. This is because justification has produced wildly varying inter-word spaces. (See 5.4, 5.5, 7.10–7.13.)

5 layout

5.1 INTRODUCTION

Although we deal with them under two chapter headings in this book, the choice of page size (see 4) and consideration of the layout of text and image cannot, in practice, be separated. For example, a multi-column grid may allow necessary flexibility in the placing of illustrations but is not compatible with a small or narrow page. So, we make the assumption in this chapter that a page format appropriate to the layout can be used. My comments about viable *text measures* (line lengths) and margins may help you to ascertain if this is so (see 5.5).

A visit to the medieval manuscript books on display at the British Library, or any major collection, will convince the would-be book designer that all that needs to be known about the relationship of text area to page was known long before printing with moveable type was thought of.

The classic proportions of inner, top, outer, and bottom margins (known before desktop publishing as back, head, fore-, and foot margins and sometimes stated ideally to be in the ratio 2 : 3 : 4 : 6) can be justified in functional terms — room to hold the book and turn the pages without obscuring the text, space to make notes in the outer margin, etc. — but the overriding factor is that they simply look right. They were more or less aspired to by makers of books from the dark ages to the middle of the nineteenth century and are still often reflected in the design of books when considerations of cost and content do not prohibit it.

Today, three factors encourage the designer to experiment with unconventional page layouts:

- the possibility of integrating all kinds of illustration with text.

- a general acceptance of the role of design in provoking and stimulating thought.

- the regrettable tendency for margins to be seen as wasted space when the cost of printing is being considered.

Left-hand page of a fourteenth-century manuscript psalter

Reproduced by courtesy of The University of Reading Department of Typography

The celebrated twentieth-century typographer and type designer, Jan Tschichold discovered that many medieval manuscript books and early printed books approximated to a grid wherein the page proportions, and those of the text area, were in the ratio 3 : 2; the text depth was equal to the page width; and the margins were in the ratio 2 : 3 : 4 : 6.

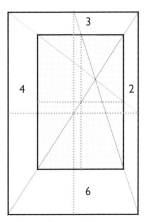

The grid to which many medieval manuscript books more or less conform. The page is both aesthetically pleasing and easy to plot with rudimentary drawing instruments.

In the following sections the word 'layout' may be taken to mean both the grid which defines text and image areas in relation to the page, and the arrangement of elements within that grid.

5.2 WHY HAVE A GRID AT ALL?

One could argue that it would be just as acceptable — or more so — to judge the size and position of the elements on every page intuitively, without reference to any underlying structure. The issues are subjective ones, as they are in most discussions involving design, and it is insufficient (although true) to say that such a process is time-consuming and therefore costly.

The most persuasive argument has to do with consideration for the reader. The first duty of the designer is to place as few obstacles as possible between the reader and the meaning of the text.

If a book is well-designed, the reader will unconsciously pick up the principles underlying the design and use them to know where to look for the text on turning the page, or to find notes and captions without consciously searching for them.

An equally good reason, which may not be as readily accepted by the sceptic, is that the structure itself can be a thing of beauty which excites interest in the book.

5.3 DOUBLE-PAGE SPREADS

The first thing that a designer must bear in mind when approaching the layout of a book is that the reader sees two pages at a time. Ignoring the effect which the arrangement of one page has on the page facing it will lead to an unsatis-factory and confusing result. The opportunity of pleasing the eye by carrying implied horizontal lines across the spread and juxtaposing or balancing elements on the two pages is there to be exploited.

An important feature to note about the open spread is the *gutter*, the centre of the spread where the pages tend to curve away from the reader and disappear into shadow. The fore-shortening of the page at the gutter means that inner or 'back' margins never appear to have quite the value you have given them and that the edges of text and pictures placed too close to the back of the page fall into the shadow.

5.4 UNITS OF MEASUREMENT

When all typographers designed books using pencils, *type-scales*, and layout paper, it was conventional to specify margins in points (approximately one seventy-second of an inch) and picas (twelve points). Type sizes, units of space, line depths, and measures were all expressed in the same units, reflecting the fact that the whole business revolved around the physical properties of metal type: this applied even after the metal type itself was replaced by images on paper and film. Pictures were at that time commonly measured in inches or millimetres, so two systems of measurement were in use at the same time, on the same layout. To add to the potential confusion, Britain and America used a different 'point' from continental Europe. You may still see references to Anglo-American or *Pica* sizes and *Didot* or *Cicero* sizes.

See 8.6.

See 7.11.

If you are using desktop-publishing software, you may be given the option of using points, inches, or millimetres. Furthermore, you may be asked whether you wish to use true picas or ones which are exactly one sixth of an inch. Despite my traditional training, I find it easier to work always in millimetres, occasionally matching older examples of typesetting by converting one pica into 4.218 mm. Everyone knows how big a millimetre is and the unit is usually small enough to allow fine positioning and sizing — very rarely you may need to use half millimetres to work at the required level of accuracy. And the decimal system gives you the best chance of manipulating picture sizes in your head. For simple books, such as novels, which are primarily text of one size, the depth of your text area may be best expressed in lines of the principal type size but for illustrated books, or books featuring text of many sizes, millimetres once again provide the most convenient unit.

5.5 MARGINS AND COLUMNS

Having decided upon your page size you need to specify margins. There can be no hard and fast rules about good and bad margins but some parameters can be determined by common sense. *Back* (or *inner*) *margins* of less than 17 mm (4 picas) should be avoided because the text or pictures will tend to disappear into the gutter (see 5.3). *Head* (*top*) *margins* and *fore-margins* (*outer margins*) will vary slightly from copy to copy because of the inaccuracy inherent in the trimming process so an allowance of about three millimetres should be

A left-hand page from a fifteenth-century Bible, printed in Germany

Reproduced by courtesy of the University of Reading Department of Typography added to what seems to be the smallest ideal margin. Because anything geometrically centred on the page will appear to be lower than the centre, the top margin should usually be less than the bottom one. Despite the problems associated with the gutter, the inner margin should be smaller than the outer one because the inner margins on facing pages will be seen together.

The margins you specify in desktop-publishing software should define the text area only. You can use moveable guides to fix the running head, folio (page number), and grid to be used for illustrations. Set all this up on 'master pages' so that it will appear on each new page as you create it.

For continuous text, there are line lengths below or beyond which text becomes a strain on the eye. If the measure is too small the spacing between words begins to vary excessively or, in the case of *unjustified* setting (see 7.12) the actual line length becomes similarly unpredictable. Just as tiring for the reader is a line so long that the eye has to travel great distances from the end of one line to the beginning of the next. As a rough guide, text measures should be between 88 mm (21 picas) and 135 mm (32 picas). For ancillary text, such as captions, notes, and subheadings, measures as short as 42 mm (10 picas) are often acceptable.

Designers working with pre-desktop-publishing tools (pen, pencil, typescale, depthscale, and layout pad) find a grid drawn in ink, so that it shows through layout paper, an indispensable aid. (See 8.5, 8.6.)

The following sample grids show the text area as a solid line and the image areas, folios and running heads as dotted lines. Examples of illustration positions are shown in grey. They are at one quarter size and are given as examples only.

Example A shows an ordinary book. There may be no illustrations and, if there are any, they will be accommodated within the single-column text grid. The page size is 245 x 172 mm, a popular size because it comes economically out of B1 and B2 paper (see 4.4) which in turn makes full use of many printers' printing machines. Apart from the typography (see 7.1 − 7.16) only the margins and the positioning of the folios and running heads give us an opportunity to make such a page interesting or elegant. In this case the margins, whilst smaller than those of the earliest printed books (*incunabula*), retain the traditional order of size.

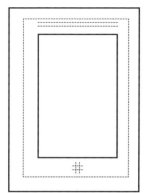

The text margins (shown here as solid lines) can be specified in the software's dialogue box. The picture grid and the positions of running head and page numbers (shown here as dotted lines) should be defined using guides on a master page.

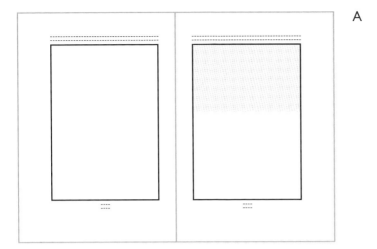

Try setting up a page of this size and filling the text area with *body type* (the meaningless pseudo-Latin text which comes with some dtp software) or any text you happen to have handy. Alter the margins and positions of the folios and running heads and see what looks good and what does not.

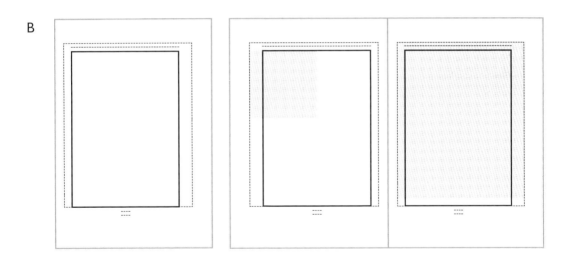

B

Example B is similar to A but some thought has been given to the needs of the illustrations. Not all the illustrations will need to occupy the full available width or height but the area is there if it is needed. Note that, although it looks acceptable to commandeer the space normally used by the running head for illustrations, to drop below the base of the text area often looks ill-judged.

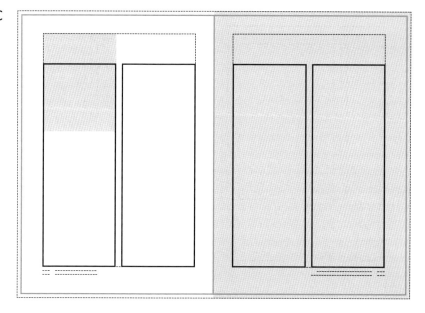

Example C shows a simple double-column grid on an A4 page (297 x 210 mm). This is a very common form of layout which allows flexibility in the treatment of the illustrations. Perhaps because it is so common, it is difficult to make two columns on A4 look inspiring. I have resorted to placing the running heads at the foot of the page and specifying a large top margin which can only be invaded by pictures. In practice, when I last used a grid like this, I found that I had to allow captions and headings to appear in the head margin and thereby lost the continuity which I had hoped the line of the top of the text area would give me. This is an illustration of the way in which the practical needs of the material can undermine the intentions of the designer. Greater flexibility in the grid and the absence of a design feature which had no practical function would have avoided the problem altogether. The space between the columns should be sufficient to separate them but not so wide that the eye has to travel great distances between them. Something between four and eight millimetres (one and two picas) is usually effective

Example D has a wide column for continuous text and a narrow one for notes, side headings, and captions. Illustrations can occupy either column or both. Again, the space between the columns should be sufficient to separate them but no more. This sort of layout can work with fairly small pages and quite large ones. Limitations are imposed by the column widths — the wide column should not be so wide as to create

unmanageably long lines of text (see 7.11, 7.12) and the narrow one should not be so narrow that many of its lines have only one or two words on them. Generally, it is a good idea to align the running heads and folios with the column which will most regularly have something in it (i.e. the wide column) — otherwise they will frequently appear to be floating randomly in space.

Example E has three columns. The page size is a slightly truncated variation on A4 (another way of making the over-familiar look interesting). A triple-column grid has the advantage of being easily adapted to a wide-column-narrow-column grid by combining two of the columns into one. For some books, flexibility of this kind between sections can be very useful.

Whatever the grid you are using, there may be occasions when the best solution to a problem is to break the rules. Text should not in general be allowed to burst out of its confines unless there is clear justification for it in the text itself, but illustrations can normally be handled with greater latitude and it is probably fair to say that the requirements of the picture always outweigh the interests of the grid.

5.6 SYMMETRICAL OR ASYMMETRICAL?

In general, books are symmetrical in the sense that the right-hand page (*recto*) grid is a mirror reflection of the left (*verso*). If you are designing a book for the first time, and there is no overriding argument against it, it makes sense to work within this tradition. There are, however, plenty of good examples of books where the effect of the design depends upon it not being symmetrical. Usually, this means that every page has the same wide-column-narrow-column grid. Asymmetrical grids were particularly favoured in the 1970s and, whilst good design outlives the period of its creation, there is a danger of unwittingly evoking the 'feel' of that decade.

Symmetry

Assymmetry

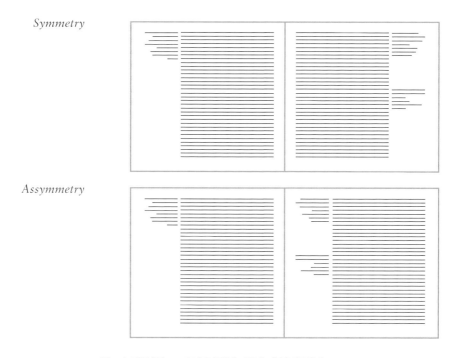

5.7 BLEEDS AND ACCURACY OF TRIMMING

Ask a binder what *tolerance* (the amount of variation one should expect) should be allowed for trimming and he will probably tell you three millimetres. It is rare for a page to be trimmed as inaccurately as this but it is better to be safe than sorry. The thickness of paper means that, in any case, the pages at the centre of a binding section have more trim taken off their foredges than those at the outside.

Because of these considerations, it is unwise to plan a grid which brings pictures too close to the page edge — ten millimetres is close enough in most cases.

By the same token, images which are meant to come right to the edge of the page must exceed that edge by three millimetres. This is called 'bleeding off' and it inevitably means that the edge of the picture will be cut off when the book is trimmed. This should be borne in mind when choosing pictures for bleeding off.

5.8 THE PLACING OF ELEMENTS WITHIN A GRID

The above notes on the virtues of different types of grid cover most aspects of the placing of text and pictures on the page. In devising the grid you will have developed ideas of where continuous text is supposed to appear, which parts of the grid can be used for pictures, how captions and headings will be positioned, and where the folios and running heads will appear. There are, however, useful underlying principles to be aware of in addition to those dictated by the grid.

Layout of text is as much a dialogue with the reader as is its content. The designer has the power to help, hinder, surprise, delight, and infuriate the reader. Clearly, only some of these reactions are desirable, though *which* ones will depend on circumstance. Each time the reader opens the book at a new place or turns the page he or she is embarking on unexplored territory. In the case of a novel, the intention of the designer should be to present the same layout as practically every other page of the book so as not to distract the reader from the continuing narrative. Only at the start of chapters or of the book as a whole is it usually permissible to delight or entertain, and the approach to those small areas of the design should be in keeping with the nature of the text.

GUIDE OR STRAIGHTJACKET?

A grid is meant to facilitate beautiful, functional pages; not to impose awkward, monotonous conformity. Always be ready to break your own rules if the occasion demands it, or because you instinctively feel that it is for the best.

Illustrated books, whether intended to inform or entertain, give far more scope for the designer to exercise his or her imagination. If the scale of illustration, or the placement of illustration and text, suddenly changes on the turning of the page, the reader's concentration will be broken and some refocusing will occur. This could be just the reaction you are looking for to emphasize a change in the subject matter or to underline an important moment of summary. In other circumstances, a designer can induce satisfaction of a different kind by always having illustrations and notes near at hand when the text causes the reader to go looking for them.

It is important always to empathize with the reader.

6 pictures

6.1 INTRODUCTION

The role of images in book design has changed in the last 150 years, with successive advances in technology, from providing occasional black-and-white line images to decorate and illustrate the text, to offering realistic, full colour glimpses of the real world or the world of the imagination, which can be as much or as little of the book as we wish. Text and image can now be fully integrated, if required, so that either becomes part of the other. And control over this process lies within the designer's computer.

Of course, not all books offer the designer an opportunity to push forward the boundaries of illustrated book design but it is valuable to be aware of the possibilities when approaching even the most modest of design problems.

6.2 GETTING PICTURES ON TO YOUR SYSTEM

If you are working with one of the industry-standard dtp programs, a *PostScript* output device, a computer with a fair amount of memory (both RAM and hard disk), a desk-top scanner, and a photo-editing program, you are in a good position to start working with images (see 8.2 and 8.4). If you are not so lucky, there are ways in which you can overcome some of the limitations of your system. If you are not using a computer at all, the present section of this book may give you an insight into the work of whoever has the job of following your specifications.

Pictures for incorporation into a book may be as simple as a single line illustration or as demanding of computer memory as a double-page colour illustration. In photographic books or art catalogues the pictures may occupy most of every page and place working with high-resolution reproduction-quality scans beyond the reach of even the well equipped designer's computer. If your scanner is a good one, you should be able to scan small line images yourself (see 6.4). Scanning tone and colour images should be left to a printer's or repro company's drum- or flatbed-scanner. The good news is that PostScript-equipped designers (i.e. those with a driver for a PostScript output device on their computer) can work with images of much lower resolution, which do not make huge demands on computer memory, then have them automatically replaced with the high-resolution ones at the output stage. You should talk to your printer about this before embarking on the design of the book.

An alternative, less satisfactory way of dealing with memory-intensive images is to produce low-resolution positional scans on your desktop scanner, then ask the printer to replace them manually with his own scans before printing (either on his computer or as pieces of film). This method does not ensure fine control of cropping and sizing but it is the only method if your computer's memory is not adequate for the task or you do not have PostScript capability.

6.3 TYPES OF IMAGE

Throughout this chapter and in your dealings with printers and repro companies, you will encounter the terms *line* and *halftone*.

Line images are composed of solid black areas on a white background. The areas might be lines or dots, giving the impression of tone, but no shades of grey are present in a line image. A scanner may be able to produce a line image from a monochrome original other than a black-and-white one (e.g. red lines on a cream background) but the result, as far as the computer is concerned, is black and white.

Part of a halftone image, magnified

Halftone images are produced by the machine which outputs the final film or plates (an imagesetter or a platesetter) from greyscale or colour scans. They translate areas of tone (i.e. shades of grey or other colours) into a fine pattern of dots, which maintain the appearance of the tones when printed.

Hold a magnifying lens over a photograph in a book or magazine to see this effect in action.

6.4 SCANNING

If you intend to use scans as final output files for printing, they need to be scanned at relatively high resolutions (2000–2800 *dots per inch* for *line* images and 350–400 *dpi* for *halftone* and colour images). Desktop scanners rarely have the level of control or quality to produce acceptable tone and colour images but, if your computer can handle the file sizes, they can often be used for line images.

Experiment will show whether you need to raise or lower the brightness level on your scanner software to get good results with line images. Generally, it needs raising for dense images with fine white lines in them, and lowering for light or faint images.

If you are having scans done for you by a repro company, always indicate any interpretation of the image which you want them to attempt. For instance, you may intend the paper on which an original tone image appears to disappear ('paper = white' or 'lose background') or solid lines in a tone image to print as if they were part of a line image ('lines = solid' or 'black lines = 100%'). You may want to draw the scanner operator's attention to a feature of the picture which requires special care (e.g. 'please retain fine lines' or 'hold detail in mid-tones'). As well as this sort of information, the scanner operator needs to know whether you intend the outcome to be a line image or a halftone, and what size you want it to be (see 6.5).

see 6.5).

LINE OR HALFTONE?

A is a line image with no shades of grey. It has been scanned as line.

B is made up of shades of grey and so has been scanned as a halftone.

C, although largely a line image, contains flat areas of grey, so must be scanned as a halftone.

D is a line image but, because of the need to hold delicate lines, both black and white, it was scanned as a halftone.

In the cases of C and D the scanner operator was asked to treat the paper background as white and the black lines as solid black. This gives the illusion of a line image.

A
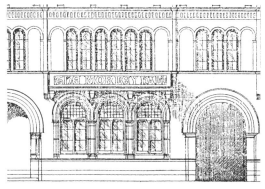

B

C

D

Drum scanners, the most common type in repro companies, require a flexible original piece of artwork (such as a photograph or transparency) which can be attached to the surface of a drum, whereas flatbed scanners can scan from rigid originals (such as bound books or mounted photographs). The cost of flatbed scanning is usually greater and some people maintain that the quality of drum scanning is higher.

Images should be saved as *TIFFs* (*Tagged-Image File Format*) or *EPSs* (*Encapsulated PostScript files*). TIFFs are often preferable for line images because they allow you to specify a transparent background at the design stage — so that a colour, another image, or type can show through. EPSs are sometimes preferred for tone images on PostScript-capable computers because they enable the designer to work with a low-resolution image (*preview*) then automatically replace it with the high-resolution image on output.

If you plan to work with low-resolution images and do not have PostScript capability, ask the scanner operator to supply high- and low-resolution files.

6.5 SIZING ILLUSTRATIONS

If you are working with dtp software on a PC or Mac, you have the ability easily to re-size pictures at the design stage. However, this cannot be done without some loss of quality. If you enlarge a 400 dpi (dots per inch) image to twice its linear size it becomes a 200 dpi image — too low a resolution for acceptable output. If you reduce an image to 50%, although the nominal resolution increases, the computer has to take tonal information which would have been represented by, say, sixteen dots and redistribute it amongst four dots. So, although a small reduction in size gives the impression of better quality, large reductions introduce undesirable distortion. As a general rule, you can re-size images to between 85% and 115% of their scanned size without fear of detectable distortion — outside that range you need a re-scan.

If you are working with *positionals* (see 6.2 above), which will eventually be replaced by high-resolution scans, it does not matter how much you re-size them on screen, provided that you can see what you are doing and that the proofs you produce will suffice.

When we speak of the size of an image in percentage terms, we are referring to linear measurements. So, if a man in a photograph is three centimetres high and you want him to print as 4.5 centimetres, the enlargement is 150%. Similarly, if a picture is 100 x 125 mm and the space you have allowed for it is 80 x 100 mm, the percentage reduction is 80%. (It may be argued that a reduction to 80% is a reduction of 20%. However, in communication between designers and printers, it is simply an 80% reduction.)

We always express image sizes as *height x width*, so 80 x 100 mm describes a picture which is wider than it is tall (*landscape*) and 100 x 80 mm is taller than it is wide (*portrait*). This rule applies equally to page sizes (see 4.7) but not to paper sizes, where the order of dimensions denotes the grain direction (see 4.6).

41 x 56 mm (landscape)

56 x 41 mm (portrait)

When specifying a size for scanning, you can give either a final dimension (e.g. 'reduce to 135 mm wide') or a percentage. The percentage method is by far the best because it allows you discretion over *masking* (or *cropping*, see 6.6) at a later stage and because it does not present a second opportunity for human error when the scanner operator converts your width or height instruction into a percentage.

To calculate a percentage, find a measurable distance in your picture (e.g. the width, the height, or something within the image such as the height of a person), divide the intended printed size of that distance by the original size (on your photograph or artwork), then multiply by a hundred.

6.6 MASKING (CROPPING)

When the area of an image which you intend to reproduce is less that the whole area, the parts which are excluded are said to be *masked off*. The process of specifying which parts are to be masked off and those which are to remain is called *masking* or *cropping*. Most software uses the term *cropping*.

In the majority of cases, cropping can be done by the designer when planning the page but, if you are specifying cropping for someone else to carry out, or if the amount of the image not to be used is very great (in which case to scan it all would be a waste of time and expense), you need to indicate accurately which parts are to be masked off. This used to be done by attaching a piece of tracing paper to the back of the artwork or photograph with masking tape, folding it over to cover the front, cutting it to the same size as the artwork, then drawing the masked area with a soft pencil and setsquare, and shading it to reveal the desired cropped image. Some text books still suggest this method, and you will find it useful if the artwork is to be protected from marking. However, the speed at which designers are expected to work today often rules it out, and you will find that most people mark masking, together with sizing information, on the back of the photograph or artwork (see 6.7).

6.7 MARKING THE ARTWORK

Line artwork with a reasonable margin on at least one edge may be marked up in soft pencil (2B–4B) on the face. Light-blue coloured pencil (which is not seen by a scanner scanning line or a camera using panchromatic film) can also be used. However, marks should always be kept outside the area to be scanned or shot on camera. Other pieces of artwork, particularly photographs, should be marked up on the back.

A number of differently treated papers are used for photographic prints and some of them are not easily marked with a pencil. If a soft pencil will not write on a photographic print, use a fine-tipped pen of the sort used for overhead projectors. Never use pens with a water-based ink, as these will permanently mark the face of any photographs with which the ink comes into contact whilst wet; always make sure the ink is dry before stacking photographs on top of each other; and never apply pressure when writing on the back of a photograph.

Before marking up artwork, delete or cross out any information relating to previous occasions upon which it appeared in print. The printer or scanner operator should not be expected to know which set of instructions to follow on the basis of handwriting analysis. The essential information for you to convey on the artwork or photograph is:

A

B

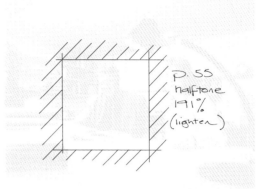

C

A *Photograph to be scanned*

B *The back of the photograph marked with masking, sizing, and other instructions*

C *The resultant scan*

- the identity of the picture. Use the filename you intend to give to the low-resolution version of the picture if you hope to replace it with the final scan automatically. The name should be unique and descriptive (e.g. ch3f4 for chapter 3, figure 4).

- the type of file you want it to be (e.g. *line, TIFF* or *h/t, EPS* — *h/t* is printers' shorthand for halftone).

- reduction or enlargement. Shorthand for 100% is *S/S* (= *same size*).

- any masking instructions. There is no need to state that nothing is to be masked off, since the scanner operator will assume this if no cropping instruction is given.

6.8 DESIGNING WITH PICTURES

The simplest way of incorporating a picture into the design of a book is to size it to the text width and place it within the text area. This may be the most appropriate style for academic books and journals where the picture is only there to illustrate

A picture sized to the text width of a book wherein the images exist primarily to illustrate the text. (In fact, elsewhere in this fairly heavily illustrated academic book pictures extend outside the text area, conforming to a grid which permits modest flexibility of treatment.)

Twentieth-Century Architecture and its Histories,
Society of Architectural Historians
of Great Britain, 2000

the text, particularly when the number of pages of text greatly exceeds the space taken up by illustration.

The opposite extreme is the picture book, or coffee-table book, where some of the pictures may cover whole pages or spreads and the role of the text may simply be to caption the pictures. In between are the majority of illustrated books, where text and images are both of importance and the needs of the pictures are not always met by confining them to the text area.

In the first case, the grid will be of the simplest kind (see 5.5, example A) and little needs to be said about the placing of pictures except that, even with the most academic of books, the designer should consider the double-page spread as the smallest visual unit. If pictures appear on facing pages, they should either align and be of the same depth or not align at all (e.g. one at the top of the page and the other at the bottom) — avoid aligning pictures which are of *slightly* different depths.

A book in which the grid serves the needs of the pictures first and the text second

An Engraver's Globe, 2002

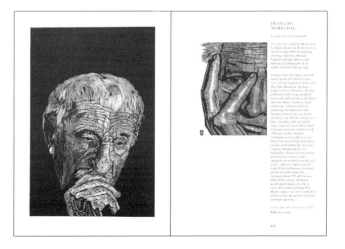

6.8.1 Picture books

Books which exist to display pictures, wherein the text occupies a secondary place, need a great deal of consideration. It is tempting to take every double-page spread entirely on its merits and, up to a point, this is the method most likely to succeed. However, both out of concern for the reader's comfort and because an element of structure is often aesthetically beneficial, it is wise to temper an intuitive approach with adherence to a grid. In such a case, the grid can be flexible and implied, rather than openly stated (see 5.5).

Remember that pictures which appear to occupy a whole page *bleed off* it by about 3 mm (see 5.7) and you must make allowance for this when sizing them.

Text on pictures

Text which overlays a picture needs to be legible, so do not place it too near the gutter (see 5.3) or so close to an edge that it is in danger of being trimmed off. If the picture behind it is dark, you should consider reversing the text out (specifying the text as white in your design, so that each character actually prints as a letter-shaped hole in the picture). If reversed-out text is too light in weight, the printer may have difficulty printing it or it may be illegible, so select a typeface for the whole book which is not too delicate. Text on a pale area of the picture should be black.

For aesthetic or practical reasons, you may sometimes wish to reverse text out of a solid black or coloured rectangle or lighten a rectangular area of a picture so that black text within it remains legible. (See note on this page.)

Text positioned within a lightened rectangular area of a picture. This is a book jacket but the device can be used to accommodate a caption within the area of a picture. Equally, text can be reversed white out of a darkened rectangle.

Francis Johnson, Architect: A Classical Statement, Oblong, 2001

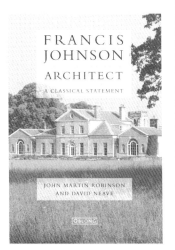

A lightened rectangle within a pictutre is achieved by the following method:

1. Open up your picture in a picture box of appropriate size. The picture must be a *TIFF*, not an *EPS*, for the trick to work.

2. Create a text box and place your text in it, arranging the text within the box as you want it to appear, with the box the size and shape of the pale area which you want to appear behind it. Make sure that the background to your text box is transparent (*none* in some software).

3. Position guide rules to align with all four sides of your text box.

4. Open another picture box the size of your text box and fitted to the guide rules, with your original picture showing in it at the same reduction or enlargement and angle of orientation as the first version of the picture.

5. Since it is smaller that the picture box, the new one will only show part of the picture. Position the picture in the new box to align exactly with the first picture, so that it appears to be a continuation of the same image.

6. Using the appropriate controls in your software, reduce the contents of the second picture box to 15% *tint* or *opacity* (experiment may suggest anything from 5% to 25%).

7. Bring the text forward (to the front) so that it shows on top of the now pale portion of the picture.

To create a cut out picture within your dtp software, do the following:

1. Open an ordinary rectangular picture box with your picture in it. Position the box and size the picture as you intend it to be (ignoring the fact that it currently has a background).

2. Start another picture box on top of the first one, this time an irregular polygonal one, and plot an edge for it to match the edge of the picture you want to cut out (this *clipping path* must be plotted with care, using very many points to define the shape).

3. Clear the original picture box so that it disappears, leaving you with an empty polygonal box.

4. Get the picture again, this time inside the box you have cut out. Make sure that it has the same reduction or enlargement as it had before, and position it to fit exactly the new box you have made for it.

Cut-out pictures with text flowing round

Cut-out pictures (*cut-outs*) are pictures with defined irregular edges and no backgrounds. They create the impression of an object standing in front of, or lying on the page. They are created by carefully drawing round the edge of the object in your photo-editing program and filling the background with white (in some software you can then convert the white to transparent) or within your dtp software by the method described in the note on this page.

Your program will give you an option for running text around objects. If you have imported a picture with a white background, run the text around the image. If you have created a shaped picture box for it (as described left), run the text around the object (the box). In either case, you will need at least a 9 pt (3 mm) gap around the picture. Experiment with margins of between 9 and 18 points (3–6 mm).

Of course, the fact that a picture is a cut-out does not mean that you must run text around it. The text may be positioned away from the picture or run across it.

Text flowing around the edge of a cut-out picture

An Engraver's Globe, 2002

6.8.2 Illustrated books

I have used the term *illustrated* to imply something different from a *picture* book. Whereas the pictures in a picture book are the body of the work, supported by small amounts of text, the pictures in an illustrated book are there to illustrate the text. The grid will be devised to present the text as a continuous thread, with the pictures either accommodated close to their references in the text or grouped in easily found locations within the book. Such a grid may need to accommodate images which extend beyond the text area (see 5.5, example B).

Before *offset lithography* came into general use, pictures were usually printed on different paper from the text. (*Letterpress* required a rough absorbent paper surface to do justice to text and line images and a glossy one to render tone and colour work.) This led to their being bound in separate sections either at the end of the book or between binding sections of text (see 1.5.3). Right up to the present day, some publishers retain this practice despite the opportunity which lithography gives them to place the pictures wherever they like.

Although logistics may occasionally demand the grouping of illustrations (when, for instance, a large number of pictures belongs with a small amount of text), your aim should be to present them to the reader at the point at which he or she needs to refer to them. This implies integrating them with the text. As is always the case, you should view the double-page spread as a unit and seek to align pictures of the same depth across the spread. Remember that the continuity of the text is important and that your design should avoid cutting it up into little pieces.

Pages from an illustrated book. The pictures make use of a picture grid which is larger than the text area. They are close to their references in the text and align with each other across the double-page spread.

Francis Johnson, Architect: A Classical Statement, Oblong, 2001

Captions

The typography of your captions (see 7) should distinguish them clearly from the text and, although your picture grid may make use of the text margin area, the captions will usually look best confined either to the text width or to a column which you have set aside especially for them (see 5.5, examples B and D).

The book you are reading makes use of a column for small pictures, notes and captions but captions appear in the text column when that provides the better solution.

6.9 OUTPUTTING IMAGES

6.9.1 Greyscale (tone) and colour images

Until they reach an output device (such as an imagesetter or a laser printer) tone pictures do not need a halftone screen. The term which dtp and graphic software uses for a black and white picture which will eventually be screened for output is *greyscale*.

Greyscale pictures, and colour pictures, must be scanned at a sufficiently high resolution to support the halftone screen which will be used to output them for printing. This means that they should be scanned so that, at their intended size, they have an *dpi* (dots per inch) resolution of about twice their intended *lpi* (lines per inch). Lines per inch is the traditional measure of the fineness of a halftone screen. Most printers use screens of between 150 and 200 lpi. For these screens, tone and colour scans should be done at between 300 and 400 dpi. Remember to tell your scanner operator what screen you intend to use for printing so that he can adjust the scanning resolution accordingly.

The choice of screen should be made in consultation with the printer and may depend as much on the paper you propose to use as on the requirements of the images themselves. As a general rule, fine screens like 200 lpi hold small details better, whilst coarser screens like 150 lpi promote better contrast.

6.9.2 Line images

Line images do not have a screen because, by definition, they are not tone images. In low-resolution line scans, curved and diagonal lines appear stepped to the naked eye. This means that the actual pixel building blocks are clearly visible giving the line a rough, fragmented appearance. To avoid this, always scan line images at 2000–2800 dpi (at their intended size).

6.9.3 Final film

After you have checked final proofs, had a set returned by the author and/or editor, and corrected them, you are ready to output the book as film or direct to printing plates (see 1.3 and 1.3.1).

Before asking a repro company to output film, check whether the printer requires positive or negative film and specify it. You should receive from the repro company (or printer) film with the pictures already in place. It is wise to check the film at this stage to make sure that none of your pictures has been missed out.

7 type and typography

7.1 INTRODUCTION

Until recently, most book designers would have considered themselves typographers. In the present age of computers and desktop-publishing software, the dividing lines between graphic designers, typographers, and compositors have become unclear. As a book designer, who still calls himself a typographer, I am now expected to produce the whole book, including illustrations, as a file, ready for outputting to film. In these circumstances, the skills of visualizing with a pencil and drawing type on layout paper can no longer be considered essential — however much a trained designer may value the experience and draw on it when making judgements.

There are, of course, considerable advantages to the modern way of working. My ideas are no longer filtered through the compositor's own set of rules and preferences: I get exactly what I specify every time — for better or for worse. And the very necessity of considering the typeface and the size has put paid to that particularly unprofessional breed of designer who would imply text by means of parallel lines of grey felt-tip pen and leave it to the printer to specify type which would fit the space delineated.

My growing experience as a typographer, from art college to the publishing and printing industries, brings with it a working knowledge of typefaces and their families which is not necessarily part of the route to desktop-publishing competence. It is, however, a vital element in a book designer's armoury and, if not acquired through physical contact with metal type and patient tracing of letter forms, must be obtained in other ways. This chapter attempts to lay the foundations for a knowledge of type, and gives some guidance for its application, but only by extensive reading and analysis of every example of printed work which catches your eye can you hope to attain proficiency and understanding.

The letter Q as it appears in the italic and roman versions of twenty different typefaces

If you are using desktop-publishing, or even word-processing software, you are probably already the owner of more typefaces (or *fonts*, see 7.2) than the average pre-computer jobbing printer would have used in his lifetime. They tend to be loaded onto your computer with the software and, although they do not all bear the names of the typefaces which they closely resemble, their names often give a clue to their parentage. (So, if you do not have Helvetica, look for a font with a name which suggests Switzerland.) Print out large-scale alphabets in some of these typefaces, particularly the ones whose names do appear in this chapter, and use them as examples for your own analysis — maybe even trace some of the characters by hand, just to get a feel for their shape.

7.2 FACE, FOUNT, AND FONT

The spelling *font*, like *program*, has come into general use because it is used by the manufacturers of computers and dtp software. There is nothing wrong with *font* unless it is that it obscures its derivation from *founding*. What is unclear is the word's exact meaning in the context of current technology.

Some people use the term *family of typefaces* to describe all those different designs (e.g. *roman*, *medium*, *bold*, *italic*, *small capitals*, *condensed*, *extended*, etc.) which bear the same name (e.g. Times or Helvetica). They would say that a *typeface* is one member of that family. The word *font*, then, would mean the typeface with all its alternative and special characters (traditionally, old-style figures, small capitals, and some commonly used signs and accented characters). Others use the word *typeface* to mean the whole set of related designs, and the word *font* to mean one of those designs (e.g. Baskerville Bold). Commercially, *font* appears to mean the smallest unit you can buy from the type foundry (e.g. Monotype, or ITC), usually a single design, such as Helvetica Bold Extended in either roman or italic, and the word *typeface* is in the process of becoming redundant.

None of this matters. The words are simply a means of making ourselves understood. The important thing is that they have the same meaning for us as they do for the person we are communicating with. For the rest of this chapter we go some way to reflecting current practice by using *typeface* to denote a family of related designs, such as Times New Roman, and *font* when we mean one of those designs (say, Times New Roman Bold Italic).

Gill Sans
Gill Sans Italic
Gill Sans Condensed
Gill Sans Light
Gill Sans Light Italic
Gill Sans Bold
Gill Sans Bold Italic
Gill Sans Bold Condensed
Gill Sans Extra Bold

Just a few of the fonts which make up Gill Sans

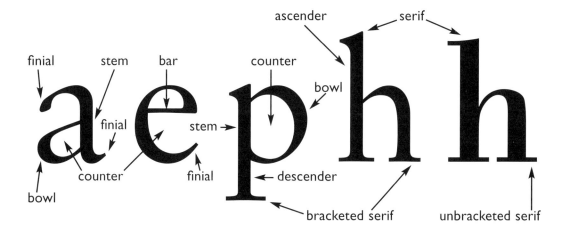

7.3 THE ANATOMY OF A CHARACTER

The figure shows the terms used in this book for the parts of a letter. The rest of this chapter makes frequent use of some of these terms so you may need to refer back to this page from time to time.

7.4 SERIF AND SANS SERIF

Serifs are the short horizontal or slanted lines at the terminals of *ascenders*, *descenders*, and *finials*. They are derived from the finishing stroke of the calligrapher's quill and the last cut of the stonemason's chisel. Typefaces which have serifs, which include all book text faces designed before the twentieth century, are called *serif* faces. Those without serifs are called *sans serifs*, sometimes abbreviated to *sans*, as in Gill Sans. The lateral emphasis of serifs helps the eye to jump the gaps between letters and keeps it from straying to other lines of type.

See 7.8.4.

Almost all typefaces are clearly serif or sans-serif faces but there are a few which are neither one nor the other. Optima is an example — truly a serif face where the serifs have been reduced to a swelling of the strokes towards their terminals, but usually classified as a sans serif.

7.5 CAPITALS AND LOWER-CASE CHARACTERS

Capital letters are sometimes called *upper case* to distinguish them from lower-case characters. The words arise from the relative positions of the metal type in the wooden type cases from which compositors hand-set type for letterpress printing.

7.5.1 Small capitals

Small capitals are capitals specially designed to have the same weight and height as lower-case letters. They are not simply capitals of a small size and their function in conventional typesetting is different. They are used, for example, in conjunction with old-style figures in post codes, for A.D. and B.C. in dates, for qualifications (B.A., PH.D., etc.), and for subheadings.

When used on their own in headings or display contexts, both capitals and *small caps* (as they are usually termed) should be generously *letter-spaced* (see 7.11).

Capital, lower-case, and small capital

7.5.2 Old-style and lining figures

Most serif typefaces were originally designed with what we now call *old-style* figures. (The notable exception is Times, which acquired old-style figures as an afterthought after it was introduced with *lining* figures). Old-style figures have the *x-height* as their basis, with several individual figures extending to the height of the *ascenders* (6 and 8) or to the depth of the *descenders* (3, 4, 5, 7, and 9).

Old-style figures

Lining figures, which are regarded as the natural companions to sans-serif typefaces, are of the same height as capitals. They are to be preferred to old-style figures, even for serif faces, when set in a line of capital letters.

Lining figures

As type founders have developed their type designs, they have frequently added lining figures to typefaces which did not originally have them, and vice versa, so that the designer often has the choice. (For examples of faces which give this choice, see Monotype Gill Sans and Baskerville.) However, although the full version of a typeface may include both forms (as well as a wider range of special characters), the version you have may not: or the software you are using may not allow you to access them. (See TrueType and PostScript fonts, 7.10.1.)

7.6 CLASSIFICATION

It is not necessary to know how to classify typefaces in order to use them. However, designers and printers need to talk to one another about type and a system of classification facilitates this. Moreover, the historic basis for type classification implies differences and similarities which help the designer to substitute faces or to pair them.

There are two distinct classification systems in use in Britain today, and both of them are subjected to frequent reinterpretation and embellishment by those who use them. The more recent, invented in France and adopted as a British Standard in 1967, uses names which are marginally more logical and comprehensible than those employed by the old system. The traditional system has evolved over centuries and the names given to the classifications are less obviously descriptive than some of those in the British Standard system. However, I have yet to meet anyone in the world of printing who uses the British Standard terms: so I have used the old terms and given the equivalent British Standard terms, where they correspond, in parentheses after them.

It is important to note at this point that, although it is possible to describe the classifications in specific terms, it is more difficult to ascribe typefaces to them because most typefaces exhibit characteristics of more than one classification. The following list is not comprehensive, concentrating as it does on those groups of typefaces which are likely to be of use to the book designer.

7.7 SERIF TYPEFACES

Centaur
Garamond

7.7.1 *Venetians and Old Faces (BS: Humanist and Garaldes, respectively)*

Two overlapping groups which display, in their lower case, characteristics of the late medieval and renaissance calligraphy from which they are derived. The emphasis of the *counters* and *serifs* is diagonal and the serifs are bracketed. Venetians, the older group, have a sloped bar to the e. In both groups, the capitals are often lower than the ascenders. [Centaur (Venetian), Monotype Garamond (Old Face)]

7.7.2 *Transitional*

Fournier
Baskerville

Called 'Transitional' because they represent a halfway stage between Old Face and Modern, these faces show the beginnings of a departure from calligraphic models towards a more mathematical reduction of letters to their essential form. This departure took place from the end of the seventeenth century to about the middle of the eighteenth. The stress of the counters and serifs is less diagonal, although not yet vertical and horizontal, and the bracketing of the serifs is less heavy. [Fournier, Baskerville]

7.7.3 Modern (BS: Didones)

Confusingly named, since they come from the mid-eighteenth century, Modern faces represent the completion of the departure from calligraphers' lettering and its replacement with rationalized mathematical forms. Modern faces are characterized by extreme contrast between thick and thin strokes, horizontal and (particularly) vertical stress, and slight or non-existent bracketing of serifs. The capital R typically has a double-curved tail and the lower-case b a serif at its foot. Popular throughout the nineteenth century in England and still widely used on the Continent, Modern faces are decidedly less legible than Old and Transitional faces and lack the even colour which many designers require of a text face, although some of them are very effective in display sizes. [Bodoni, Scotch Roman]

7.7.4 Egyptian or Slab-serif (BS: Mechanistic)

Faces derived from nineteenth-century display faces and having serifs of a similar weight to the strokes of the letter. They fall into two subcategories: those with some variation in stroke width and bracketed serifs (e.g. Clarendon) and those with even stress and unbracketed serifs (e.g. Rockwell).

7.7.5 Glyphic or Incised

This is not a traditional classification, perhaps because the typefaces which belong to it are relatively recent. Glyphic typefaces take their character from stonecutters' letters. [Perpetua, Albertus]

7.8 SANS-SERIF TYPEFACES

Classified traditionally simply as 'sans serif' and called 'lineal' in the British Standards system, sans-serif faces can be further subdivided. Because the old classification only recognises two subcategories, we use the British Standard ones, of which there are four: Grotesque, Neo-Grotesque, Geometric, and Humanist.

7.8.1 Grotesque

Based on early nineteenth-century display faces, Grotesques have variable stress and non-geometric bowls. The original Grotesques are not much used in book design. [Monotype Grotesque, Headline Bold]

Bodoni

Scotch

Roman

ob

Clarendon

Rockwell

Perpetua

Albertus

Grotesque

Headline Bold

Univers

Helvetica

7.8.2 Neo-Grotesque

Twentieth-century faces with some similarity to Grotesques, but designed with pleasing subtlety of shape and evenness of colour for text setting. Carefully leaded and in the right context, these typefaces can be effective text faces. [Univers, Helvetica]

7.8.3 Geometric

Futura

Arising from design theories current in the 1920s and 30s (especially those of the Bauhaus), these faces make no concession to the traditions of proportion and emphasis which had characterised most successful text faces since the invention of moveable type, substituting simple geometric shapes — sections of circles and vertical lines of even thickness. As one might expect, they are not, as a class, remarkably legible. However they can be arresting and attractive when used with restraint and where continuous reading is not the first requirement. [Futura]

7.8.4 Humanist

Optima

Gill Sans

As its name implies, this group of sans-serif typefaces has an affinity with Venetian or Old-face serif faces and inherits some of their superior legibility. Optima, mentioned above, belongs to this category and Eric Gill's extremely successful family of Gill Sans attempts to combine both Geometric and Humanist virtues. [Optima, Gill Sans]

OHTPEabdegjq

Gill Sans: Geometric capitals with largely Humanist lower-case

7.9 TYPOGRAPHY: MAKING A START

The first part of this chapter dealt with the way we describe and classify type. There is much more to know about the history of typefaces and the relationship between type design and other aspects of art and thought. It is beyond the scope of this handbook to examine these important subjects, but further study is highly recommended and will increase your scope and effectiveness as a designer. The following subsections deal with ways in which you can use the knowledge you have acquired and offer some general guidelines to increase your chances of success as you start to experiment.

7.10 CHOOSING A TYPEFACE

7.10.1 *TrueType and PostScript typefaces*

Most computers come equipped with a choice of typefaces. Windows and MacOS themselves provide a small selection: your word-processor and desktop-publishing software will offer you a much wider choice. Thousands of typefaces can be bought on a single CD-Rom for very little money. Most of these free or very cheap typefaces are what are known as *scaleable* or *TrueType* fonts. These fonts will produce a satisfactory result if your aim is merely to produce a tidy publication — say, for example, a newsletter or a small trader's price list — but for typographic excellence and sustained legibility you should really obtain *PostScript* faces.

If your aim is to design a book the old-fashioned way, with pens, pencils, and a layout pad, you should first discover what typefaces your typesetter or printer has or establish that he is prepared to order the face of your choice.

As you become familiar with more and more typefaces you will begin to notice features of them which facilitate quick recognition. The following list gives pointers for recognising a few of the most useful and commonly encountered faces as well as providing brief notes about their derivation, classification, and possible uses.

7.10.2 *Some useful typefaces described*

Baskerville [Transitional]

Faces of this name, from a number of foundries, are based on the eighteenth-century faces of John Baskerville. Baskerville is very legible in most sizes and is widely used. Perhaps because we are over-familiar with it, it seems to lack character and elegance, but the capital Q and many of the Italic capitals have a degree of flourish (these italic capitals are called swash caps). Although not unique to Baskerville, the spur at the top of the italic p, the italic Z which terminates below the base-line, and the vertical serifs of the capital S are features to look out for. Baskerville is an all-purpose text face which is appropriate when clarity is the overriding requirement (e.g. in a text book).

Faces of this name, from a number of companies, are based on the eighteenth-century faces of John Baskerville. *Baskerville is very legible in most sizes and is widely used.*

Bembo [Old Face]

Based on a late fifteenth-century typeface of Francesco Griffo, used by Aldus Manutius in Cardinal Bembo's *de Aetna*, Bembo

Q f y g
R r e a
R & &

Based on a late fifteenth–century typeface of Francesco Griffo, used by Aldus Manutius in Cardinal Bembo's *de Aetna*, Bembo is an elegant face, *comparatively light in overall appearance, with particularly fine serifs.*

ERga
AWzy

The archetypal Modern, Bodoni is based on the typefaces of Giambattista Bodoni (1740–1813) *and owes even less to Old face and Transitional forms than does Scotch Roman.*

ThRaj
Fqawy

Fournier was a book designer, type designer, type founder, and printer, who flourished in the middle of the eighteenth century. His typefaces

is an elegant face, comparatively light in overall appearance, with particularly fine serifs. The italic is a Chancery italic (so-called because it is derived from the chancery script of fifteenth-century Italian officials) with a long lower-case f, a serif on the descender of the y, and attractive capitals. The roman R, in some versions of the face, has a sharp, elongated tail, which looks distinctive but creates spacing problems in display lines of all caps. The R in versions of Bembo which are based on those designed for Linotype or Intertype hot-metal typesetting machines has a tail which is shorter though equally sharp. Because of its light weight and spindly serifs, Bembo does not fare as well in offset lithography as it did in the days of letterpress printing (wherein the ink spreads slightly on impact with the paper, adding weight to the characters). However, it is still a fine face, particularly when elegance is more important than sustained legibility. Properly spaced, the capitals are pleasing in display sizes.

Bodoni [Modern]

The archetypal Modern, Bodoni is based on the typefaces of Giambattista Bodoni (1740–1813) and owes even less to Old face and Transitional forms than does, for example, Scotch Roman. Bodoni's serifs are unbracketed and thin. Its emphatically vertical stress is both its strength and its handicap. The individual letters are pleasingly designed and, despite the exaggerated contrast between thick and thin strokes, the weight is consistent across capitals and lower-case. However, in text setting the effect is dazzling and tiring on the eye. Try using Bodoni as a display face in combination with dissimilar faces and, if you cannot avoid using it for text setting, space the lines (see 7.11, *leading*) as much as you dare to counteract its verticality.

Fournier [Transitional]

Fournier was a book designer, type designer, type founder, and printer, who worked in the middle of the eighteenth century. His typefaces were narrower and more rationalized than those of his contemporaries. The Monotype face which bears his name is one of two which were produced in the 1920s from Fournier's type specimens of 1742: the other is Barbou. Fournier is a clear, legible face, identifiable by its short capitals (as compared with the ascenders); its low x-height; and italic y, the descender of which curls suddenly after starting as a straight, diagonal line. The top of the italic y curves outwards and in this, as in other details, it presages Modern faces like Bodoni. Very popular as a book typeface in Britain just after it was introduced by Monotype, it has been overlooked in recent times, although it may now be embarking on a revival. It needs to be set in reasonably large sizes (e.g. 11 or 12 point) but does not require a great amount of *leading*.

Garamond [Old Face]

There are many faces called Garamond and they do not all bear a strong resemblance to the Monotype and Stempel versions, which might be thought to be among the best. As a hot-metal book typeface for letterpress printing, Garamond had no equal where a combination of grace and legibility was needed. The Monotype roman was based on an early-seventeenth-century typeface of Jean Jannon; the italic on a mid-sixteenth century face by Robert Granjon. It was easily recognised by two features: its 'cupped' serifs and the different angles of inclination of its capital and lower-case italic characters. Today's PostScript Garamonds lack some of the eccentricity of the hot-metal face. The cupped serifs seem less extreme and the slope of the Italic has been regularized. As with so many great metal typefaces, the absence of ink-spread in lithography means that the appearance of the type is less substantial. Despite these shortcomings, it remains an attractive and useful book typeface. If you have the Monotype version, you can use it in quite small sizes (at least half a point smaller than Fournier, for instance, for the same effect). The italic, in particular makes a good display face, but in large sizes you will need to alter the *letter-spacing* (*kerning*).

Gill Sans [unclassifiable sans serif]

Sculptor, stone-cutter, wood-engraver, and letterer, Eric Gill abandoned his training as an architect and took up stone-cutting and lettering, apprenticing himself for the latter to Edward Johnston. The combined influence of cutting letters with a chisel and studying with Edward Johnson account for a large part of the character of Gill's type designs. The only face which Gill Sans resembles at all is Johnson's London Transport face, which can still be seen on the London Underground. Once seen, Gill Sans will always be recognised — almost everything about it is distinctive. I would suggest as a starting point its Geometric capitals set beside its Humanist lower case and italic. Typically, Gill's italics are sloped roman characters, and none more so than Gill Sans italic. Gill Sans comes in a huge

were narrower and more rationalized than those of his contemporaries. *The Monotype face which bears his name is one of two which were produced in the 1920s from his type specimens.*

WTapf
AGgpyw
W& n

There are many faces called Garamond and they do not all bear a strong resemblance to the Monotype and Stempel versions, which might be thought to be among the best. *As a hot-metal book typeface for letterpress printing, Garamond had no equal where a combination of grace and legibility was needed.*

[MONOTYPE GARAMOND]

TOTOT
TOQGfg
akQGfgak

Sculptor, stone-cutter, wood-engraver, and letterer, Eric Gill abandoned his training as an architect *and took up stone-cutting and lettering, apprenticing himself for the latter to Edward Johnston.*

EGagyt
OWagyt
&&1234

A broad family of
sans-serif fonts,
which rivals Frutiger's
Univers, *Helvetica
was designed by M.
Miedinger.*

J P G W Q
a n j y k g
Q K P G &
a n w g y k p

Another Eric Gill
typeface, copied by
Monotype from a face
cut for Gill by H. W.
Caslon, *Joanna has an almost
Old-face roman and a typical
Gill, sloped-roman italic.*

PgxQpay

A twentieth-century
typeface which has the
characteristics of an
Old-face design. *The
italic is a similarly
orthodox Chancery italic.*
[PALATINO LIGHT]

R W U J a p
P w u a f g y

The face which most
betrays Eric Gill's back-
ground, *Perpetua has fine,
sharpened serifs and a
relatively small x-height.*

range of weights and variations, many of which were designed by Gill or had his blessing and most of which are available as PostScript fonts.

Helvetica [Neo-Grotesque]

A broad family of sans-serif fonts, which rivals Frutiger's Univers, Helvetica was designed by M. Miedinger. If you have Univers in your armoury of typefaces you may not need Helvetica (and vice-versa). For a description of Univers and a tip for distinguishing between these two useful typefaces, see below.

Joanna [unclassifiable serif]

Another Eric Gill typeface, copied by Monotype from a face cut for Gill by H. W. Caslon, Joanna has an almost Old-face roman and a typical Gill, sloped-roman italic. The lack of contrast between thick and thin strokes gives it a quirky, slightly awkward appearance which may reduce its legibility. Paradoxically, it is the same quality which makes it attractive and memorable. On first acquaintance, Joanna's extremely narrow italic is its most distinctive aspect. Notable characters include the T with its exaggerated vertical serifs and the lower-case italic g, which looks like a written g (see also Perpetua and Gill Sans). Joanna is currently enjoying a revival of interest, and deservedly so. Try using it in combination with Gill Sans (see above).

Palatino [Old Face]

A twentieth-century typeface which has the characteristics of an Old-face design. The italic is a similarly orthodox Chancery italic. The designer, Hermann Zapf, had a feeling for calligraphic forms which rendered his designs almost too emphatically aesthetic. Palatino has frequently been used successfully as a book text face. My own feeling is that it has more obvious strengths as a display face.

Perpetua [Glyphic]

The face which most betrays Eric Gill's stone-cutting background and, probably, his most successful legacy, Perpetua has fine, sharpened serifs and a relatively small x-height. Like Gill's other faces, it sacrifices legibility for purity of form but, set in large sizes (e.g. 12 pt or 13 pt) with little or no leading, it is an elegant and practical text face. The 'sloped roman' italic has flamboyant f, y and capital Q and the roman capital U has a final spur like an enlarged lower-case u.

Plantin [Old Face]

Based on type from the Plantin Museum in Antwerp, designed in the sixteenth century by Robert Granjon, Plantin would once have been called an 'Old Dutch' face. Such faces were in widespread use in Europe before Fournier and Baskerville designed what we now call their 'Transitional' faces. Plantin is a heavy face, even in its lighter 'Book' variant, and well suited to printing on rough and uncoated papers. In conjunction with its general heaviness, particularly evident in the bowls of the lower-case c and e, it can be recognised by the gap at the bottom of the bowl of its capital P (although this is a feature which it shares with some more elegant typefaces). Plantin is less used now than it was in the days of letterpress printing.

Sabon [Old Face]

Resembling Palatino only insofar as it is a twentieth-century face with Old-face characteristics, Sabon was designed by Jan Tschichold for simultaneous production, both as a metal face and as a filmset one, by Monotype, Linotype, and Stempel. It manages this feat of universality whilst remaining an example of elegance and legibility. It has relatively narrow, attractive capitals and a large x-height, and is most readily identified by its italic f, which is abruptly cut off at the bottom of the descender to make it suitable for Linotype hot-metal machines (which could not accommodate a character which overlapped the body of an adjacent one). If you own or specify Sabon, you may well find it to be the most useful typeface in your repertoire. (*The text of this book is set in Sabon.*)

Times New Roman [Transitional]

Times New Roman, usually simply called Times, was designed by Stanley Morison in 1932 for *The Times* newspaper. To fulfil its brief, it needed to work well when printed on to newsprint (the paper of which newspapers are made) and to be legible in the small sizes used for *Times* classified advertisements. In similar circumstances it would still be a good choice. Unfortunately, a version of it is the default serif typeface supplied with most computers and, as such, appears in many amateur (and ill-considered professional) publications when a different typeface would have been more appropriate. This phenomenon, combined with the fact that many of us encountered it in our

PKGW
asqcje
fKsowz

Based on type from the Plantin Museum in Antwerp, designed in the sixteenth century by Robert Granjon, *Plantin would once have been called an 'Old Dutch' face.*

SPRafsk
PQyhfp

Resembling Palatino only insofar as it is a twentieth-century face with Old-face characteristics, *Sabon was designed by Jan Tschichold for simultaneous production, as both a metal face and a filmset one.*

TheKJ
NnMm
AQpjf

Times New Roman, usually simply called Times, was designed by Stanley Morison in 1932 for *The Times* newspaper. *To fulfil its brief, it needed to work well when printed onto newsprint (the paper of which newspapers are made) and to be legible in the small sizes used for* Times *classified advertisements.*

[8 ON 9 PT TIMES NEW ROMAN]

EGagyt OWagyt &&1234

ital

Designed in 1957 by Adrian Frutiger, the Univers family of fonts is the most widely used of sans-serif typefaces. *It arose from inter-war Bauhaus ideas about purity of form, but incorporates variety of stress to promote legibility and to counter distortions of shape brought about by letterpress printing.*

a

[Helvetica]

a

[Univers]

childhood as a school textbook face, results in a level of over-exposure which makes it difficult to assess on its merits. It is recognizable by its sharp serifs and exceptionally large x-height, and would probably benefit from not being used for a decade or so.

Univers [Neo-Grotesque]

Designed in 1957 by Adrian Frutiger, the Univers family of fonts is the most widely used of sans-serif typefaces. It arose from inter-war Bauhaus ideas about purity of form, but incorporates variety of stress to promote legibility and to counter distortions of shape brought about by letterpress printing. Univers is available in a bewildering range of weights and variations, each of which is identified by a number. Univers 55, 65, and 75 represent suitable light, medium and bold faces, together with their italic equivalents, 56, 66, and 76. The oval (rather than circular) shape of the lower case letters makes it easy to tell Univers from Gill Sans (a typeface of entirely different character). A more difficult distinction to make is that between Univers and Helvetica, a similarly extensive family of faces. The most definite point of difference, albeit a small one, is the curve on the bottom finial of the Helvetica lower-case a, which is absent in Univers. Although infrequently appropriate as a text face, in their elegant light weights and in their distinctive extended and condensed forms, both Univers and Helvetica can be very useful. (Try them, for instance, for subheadings or captions, used alongside a serif face like Sabon.)

7.10.3 *Which typefaces to use*

There is no rule about which typeface is most suitable for which application. Much depends upon your own taste and allegiances — and, although we all like to think of ourselves as beyond its influence, fashion does a great deal to shape our choices. There are, however, practical considerations which hold good in all circumstances. These can be summarized under three headings: *Legibility*, *Appearance*, and *Economy*.

Legibility

The first task of a designer is a negative one: not to place any obstacle between the author's text and the reader. This may appear obvious but it is the point of failure for much professional design and cannot be emphasised too strongly when you approach design for the first time. Having taken this principle on board, we should go further and say that the designer should conspire with the author to facilitate the reader's understanding of the text. One element in meeting this challenge is the selection of a typeface which is sufficiently legible.

Why not, then, determine which is the most legible face and use it all the time? In the above descriptions I have used the word *legible* about as often as I have used the word *elegant*, and not always to describe the same typeface. The book which you are designing may involve substantial passages of text requiring continuous reading (e.g. a novel or a language text book), in which case the need for legibility is paramount. On the other hand, it may be a heavily illustrated 'coffee-table' book or a reference work, neither of which requires sustained reading: in these cases the attractiveness of the page and its impact on the reader's eye may vie with legibility for primacy.

Serifs aid legibility, as does a large x-height in smaller sizes. Evenness of 'colour' could also be said to make reading easier. Typefaces notable for their legibility include Times, Garamond, and Sabon.

Appearance

Attractiveness and legibility are not mutually exclusive. Both should be in the mind of the designer at all times. It is a question of emphasis, and some typefaces are more emphatically attractive than they are legible. Design for appearance is not always, in any case, a matter of attractiveness. Impact, emphasis, dramatic effect: these things may be achieved by typography which, in other circumstances, might be thought positively unattractive.

Leaving aside the use of type to startle or impress the reader, you might wish to select one of the less legible faces, such as Perpetua, Bodoni, or the sans serifs, for a book, or parts of a book, where small amounts of text are to be taken separately (such as the definitions in a dictionary or the notes and references in an academic book) or are associated with illustrations (e.g. captions where the text face is a contrasting, more legible one; or the text of picture books, such as travel guides and art books).

Economy

Economy in book design may be economy either of space or of expense, and is often of both. It is rare for a designer to be allowed to work outside the confines of cost-effectiveness. Budgets may be fixed or a viable selling price might impose limits on the cost of production. Since it has become common for the author to supply his or her text on disk, the quantity of type has had less bearing on cost than the number of pages. So, it has become even more important to publishers to squeeze as many words onto the page as possible. (As a designer, you should hope that *possible* means *consistent with good design*.)

Another reason for economy may arise from the function of the book. A pocket reference book, to be used at work or on the move, needs to be of handleable size in terms of both page dimensions and number of pages. Here, a typeface which is legible in small sizes, such as Times or Plantin, is essential.

One face which combines the qualities of legibility, elegance, and economy is Sabon.

7.11 SIZE, LEADING, AND SPACING

There are two 'point' systems for describing the relative size of type within a family of fonts — Cicero, or Didot, (the continental European system) and Pica (the Anglo-American system). Both are based on a measure called a 'point' and both approximate to six 12-point lines to the inch. In Didot a point is .0148″ (.376 mm): in Anglo-American it is .0138″ (.351 mm). The point size of type describes the height of the metal body on which the type was cast before the days of filmsetting and digitization — it is equal to slightly more than the distance from the top of the ascenders to the bottom of the descenders.

Because of differences in the internal proportions of type-faces (e.g. the x-height relative to the height of the ascenders) it is not sufficient to compare the appearing size of two typefaces by referring to their point sizes. However, as a general rule, it is fair to say that 8 pt to 8.5 pt type is suitable for footnotes, references, and indexes; 9 pt to 11 pt for captions and extracted quotations; and 10 pt to 13 pt for text. (For reader-comfort, aim to have no more than thirteen words on an average line of your text size.) Subheadings may be in the same size as the text or a little larger, and display type (everything from chapter headings to the title page) could be in any size from a little larger than the text size up to very large sizes such as 72 pt.

For letterpress printing from cast type, the body of the type determined the closest positioning of one character against another, both horizontally and vertically. Because it was physically impossible for the type to be set closer (except in the case of display type, which was sometimes shaved in order to *kern*

Opposite page: Times and Perpetua set in sizes which you might use for footnotes, quotations or captions, and text. Note that, because of the relationships of their x-heights to the heights of their ascenders, different nominal sizes of the two typefaces appear similar.

Because of differences in the internal proportions of typefaces (e.g. the x-height relative to the height of the ascenders) it is not sufficient to compare the appearing size of two typefaces by referring to their point sizes. However, as a general rule, it is fair to say that 8 pt to 8.5 pt type is suitable for footnotes, references, and indexes; 9 pt to 11 pt for captions and extracted quotations; and 10 pt to 13 pt for text.

Times New Roman
8 on 9 pt

Because of differences in the internal proportions of typefaces (e.g. the x-height relative to the height of the ascenders) it is not sufficient to compare the appearing size of two typefaces by referring to their point sizes. However, as a general rule, it is fair to say that 8 pt to 8.5 pt type is suitable for footnotes, references, and indexes; 9 pt to 11 pt for captions and extracted quotations; and 10 pt to 13 pt for text.

Times New Roman
9 on 11 pt

Because of differences in the internal proportions of typefaces (e.g. the x-height relative to the height of the ascenders) it is not sufficient to compare the appearing size of two typefaces by referring to their point sizes. However, as a general rule, it is fair to say that 8 pt to 8.5 pt type is suitable for footnotes, references, and indexes; 9 pt to 11 pt for captions and extracted quotations; and 10 pt to 13 pt for text.

Times New Roman
11 on 13 pt

Because of differences in the internal proportions of typefaces (e.g. the x-height relative to the height of the ascenders) it is not sufficient to compare the appearing size of two typefaces by referring to their point sizes. However, as a general rule, it is fair to say that 8 pt to 8.5 pt type is suitable for footnotes, references, and indexes; 9 pt to 11 pt for captions and extracted quotations; and 10 pt to 13 pt for text.

Perpetua 9 on 10 pt with old-style figures

Because of differences in the internal proportions of typefaces (e.g. the x-height relative to the height of the ascenders) it is not sufficient to compare the appearing size of two typefaces by referring to their point sizes. However, as a general rule, it is fair to say that 8 pt to 8.5 pt type is suitable for footnotes, references, and indexes; 9 pt to 11 pt for captions and extracted quotations; and 10 pt to 13 pt for text.

Perpetua 10 on 11 pt with old-style figures

Because of differences in the internal proportions of typefaces (e.g. the x-height relative to the height of the ascenders) it is not sufficient to compare the appearing size of two typefaces by referring to their point sizes. However, as a general rule, it is fair to say that 8 pt to 8.5 pt type is suitable for footnotes, references, and indexes; 9 pt to 11 pt for captions and extracted quotations; and 10 pt to 13 pt for text.

Perpetua 13 on 14 pt with old-style figures

certain character pairs) this position represented something closer than the ideal, particularly vertically. For ease of reading, it was usually necessary to add space between the lines. Interlinear spacing is called *leading* because strips of type metal (which contains lead) were used to keep the lines of type apart. Type without leading is said to be *set solid* or its size is expressed as a particular body size (e.g. 10 point) over the same line depth — so, *10 on 10 point* type is the same as *10 point solid*. Since type foundries have been freed from the physical constraints of metal, one cannot even be sure that the descenders and ascenders of solid type will not overlap and, at best, it can be hard to read. So, you will normally need to lead text type a little.

10 on 11 or *10 on 12 point* are common text sizes (the first being 1-point leaded and the second 2-point). For a typeface with a large x-height, such as Times, you may need more leading (say *10 on 13.5 point*) — for a small-x-height, long-ascender-and-descender face like Perpetua, a smaller amount of leading may need to be offset by a larger body size (say *11 on 11.5 point*). Type-size and leading are usually written as fractions — so *10 on 12 pt Times* is written as '$^{10}/_{12}$ Times'.

Exaggerated leading, like *11 on 16 point*, imparts a sense of luxury to some typefaces in some circumstances: but such things are matters of fashion and a design which depends on them for its success may quickly appear dated.

If you are using a computer to design, you can experiment with different amounts of leading before letting anyone else see what you have done.

The horizontal space between characters is a question of greater subtlety. It used to be called *letter-spacing*, and the practice of shaving metal characters to bring them closer together was called *kerning*. Nowadays, it is all called either *kerning* or *tracking*. Tracking is the application of letter-spacing, wider or narrower than the default, to a large amount of text. Kerning is the adjustment of letter spacing between individual pairs of letters.

Trial and error will help you to decide whether tracking is necessary. Different desktop-publishing programs give different levels of control over tracking. The one I use gives units down to decimals of a point: some others offer preset options like 'tight' and 'loose'. In my experience, most PostScript typefaces need some positive tracking to avoid the letters appearing crowded together. The object should be to achieve an all-over unity of tone (*greyness* or *colour*) across the page and to help the reader by allowing the words to stand as units whilst not requiring the eye to jump yawning gaps between them.

Kerning is used for type in display sizes because letter spacing which works for text sizes appears too crude, and often too loose, when enlarged. Look at the shapes of the letters and try to determine which combinations are 'capturing' too much space between them, and which need a little more.

Capitals are designed with sufficient space around them to work when they are used in combination with lower-case letters (as at the start of a proper noun or a sentence). This space is not sufficient to separate them when they are used on their own. It has, therefore, always been good practice to letter-space capitals and small capitals. As with other forms of tracking and kerning, trial and error will teach you how much space is needed. In display sizes, generous tracking often gives good results.

7.12 JUSTIFICATION

An important decision to make when considering the layout of a book (see 5) is whether the type should be justified. *Justification* of type used to mean setting it with all the lines the same length, so that you have a well-defined, straight edge down each margin: the alternatives being to *range it left* (so that the left-hand margin is defined by a straight line but the right-hand margin is *ragged*), to *range it right* (producing a ragged left-hand margin), or to *centre* it (neither margin being straight). In more recent times, *justification* has come to mean the whole question of which of these options to go for — but there is still no better word than *justified* to describe the first.

For the setting of most text, we need only consider the first two: justified text and ranged-left text. It may be sufficient in many circumstances that neat or ragged margins appeal to you, but there are sometimes practical reasons for opting for one or the other and these should be examined.

Two phenomena must be considered (and they tend towards opposing conclusions). One is the distance the eye has to travel between the end of one line and the start of the next, and the other is the gap to be traversed between one word and the next. In terms both of their size and of their regularity, these distances can be distracting, even tiring, for the reader.

In the case of justified text, the distance between the ends and beginnings of lines is always the same — a good thing — and, if the *measure* (the length of the line) is reasonably long,

SPACING DISPLAY TYPE

The space 'captured' between the characters (here indicated approximately in grey) should appear as even as possible. Capitals require extra space, whilst lower-case characters often need *negative kerning*.

woollen

TRAWL

BRAVADO

The word BRAVADO is shown above with the same letter-spacing between each pair of characters.

The result is that it reads as BR AVA D O. By adjusting the individual spaces we can avoid the apparent breaking up of the word:

BRAVADO

See 4.8.

the inter-word spaces will not vary greatly either — also a good thing. The measure can be *too* long, however, making heavy work for the reader's eyes (anything over 32 picas, 135 mm, will cause strain).

In such a case, you may decide to divide the text area into two columns, creating a narrow measure. Because there are rules about the breaking of words, limiting the points at which it is permitted to end a line, text justified to a narrow measure necessitates large and widely varying word spaces — causing even more discomfort to the reader than uneven line endings.

The natural conclusion is that, whilst justified type may be preferred for wide measures, ranged left (unjustified, ragged) text is better for narrow ones. Where to draw the line between narrow and wide measures will depend on the size of the type, the overall layout of the page, and the nature of the text — but, as a rule of thumb, above 25 picas (105 mm) is wide and below 20 picas (84 mm) is narrow.

7.13 HYPHENATION

Word-processing and desktop-publishing software allows the user some degree of control over the way words split at the ends of lines. Typographers have rules which they apply to this problem and it is useful to be aware of them. Whether you attempt to make the software follow your rules or turn off the program's automatic hyphenation altogether and split the words yourself is a choice for you to make each time you embark on a new book. Many designers, myself included, consider automatic hyphenation unsatisfactory and prefer to do the job manually.

Splitting words at the end of unjustified (ragged) lines is rightly frowned upon but may have to be considered where a narrow measure leads to wildly varying line lengths.

7.13.1 *Length of word-part remaining*

When a word breaks at the end of a line, a portion of it remains on the line and the rest is taken over. Most software defaults to allowing as little as two characters to form either part (as in *ad-vent* or *past-ed*). I invariably set the minimum at three characters (so neither *advent* nor *pasted* can be split). You may also wish to set the minimum length of word which can be considered for splitting. Logically, if you have not permitted two-character word-parts the minimum must be six characters. (Even if you are inclined to allow words to break before or after two characters, you would be well advised not to permit the splitting of four- or five-letter words.)

Hyphens at the end of more than three successive lines should never be allowed, and more than two should be avoided wherever possible.

7.13.2 Permissible breaks

The rules governing permissible word-splits are too numerous to list in this book. It is advisable to have a good spelling and hyphenation dictionary to hand at all times (see 10) in case common sense or your software's hyphenation dictionary does not provide an acceptable answer. The two principal bases for approaching the question are *pronunciation* and derivation and it should be emphasised that neither provides an adequate set of rules on its own.

Pronunciation

Consider the difference between *archae-ol-ogy* and *archaeo-logical* (the proposed breaks are taken from a hyphenation dictionary). The derivation is the same but the points at which the words break are different. You may not agree with this particular example (hyphenation is a subject upon which opinions differ) but you will be able to think of examples of your own. The aim is to avoid presenting the reader with part of a word which leads him or her to mentally mispronounce the whole. Two useful rules which have pronunciation as their basis are: split between double consonants (e.g. *sup-pose*) and split after the *a* in words ending in *ation* (e.g. *organiza-tion*).

Derivation

Suggesting that a designer apply rules arising from derivation presupposes that he or she has some idea of where words come from and which parts of them constitute detachable prefixes and suffixes. If you do not feel confident about this, ignore the rest of this paragraph and refer to your hyphenation dictionary. It is frequently helpful, when hyphenating words to dismantle them according to their derivation (e.g. *Anti-dis-establish-ment-arian-ism*), but this method should not be followed blindly if it leads to mispronunciation.

There is a further rule worth bearing in mind: avoid breaking a word into other, misleading, words (e.g. *the-rapist*, *read-just*).

7.14 PAGE AND COLUMN BREAKS

The rules which determine what is an acceptable page- or column-break fall somewhere between editorial style (see 9) and typography but, whoever has the responsibility of deciding them, the designer needs to know what they are.

There are some rules which are so much a matter of convention that your desktop-publishing software defaults to

widow

orphan

them. Others are more a matter of taste and refinement. Look in your program's preferences menus for phrases like *keep lines together* or *allow widows*. This setting allows you to permit or prohibit what are called *widow* and *orphan* (or *club*) lines — the last (*widow*) or first (*orphan*) line of a paragraph remaining on its own at the top or bottom of a page. Orphan lines and, more particularly, widow lines are considered unacceptable mainly because they break up the shape of the text area. They also send out a signal to the reader (although he or she may not be conscious of it) that this is amateur and ill-considered typesetting. The short page resulting from disallowing widows and orphans can be remedied by increasing or decreasing the number of lines in a nearby paragraph (by the subtle use of tracking or kerning, or by forcing a line to break at a point before its natural end) or adjusting the space above and below subheadings in the vicinity of the page break.

The other thing which your software may allow you to preset is the acceptability or otherwise of hyphens at the ends of columns and pages. Again, you would be best advised simply to prohibit them.

However, there are circumstances in which you may need to permit occasional orphan lines and broken words. For instance, there may be no other way to obtain even column- or page-depths than to permit an orphan line — or you may decide that the need for economy or speed requires you to allow words to break at the end of columns or across a double-page spread but not between one spread and the next. These things are best achieved by setting the software to follow your ideal rules then breaking them yourself in particular instances. If that proves impossible in practice, the alternative is to set low standards for the software then correct the worst offences manually. Either way, it is better to know the rules and break them than not to be conscious of them at all.

7.15 SPACES AND DASHES

7.15.1 *Spaces*

variable space

ennspace

en space

emMspace

em space

There are two forms of space instantly available to the user of most dtp software: the variable space obtained by hitting the space bar, and the *en* space (equivalent to the width of an average lower-case letter) obtained on a Macintosh computer by *alt–space* and on a PC by using the *insert special character* function. (These generalizations may not apply to all software.) In addition, you can obtain an *em* space (twice the size of an en space and approximately equal to the width of a capital M) by keying two en spaces.

Designers have traditionally been able to call on a number of smaller fixed spaces of which the *thick* space (a third of an em) and the *thin* space (an eighteenth of an em) were the most useful. You can imitate the effect of these smaller spaces by using positive kerning.

En and em spaces are most frequently used as separators: for instance, after the number in a numbered subheading or before the page number in a contents list. When setting numbers in columns (e.g. in tables or accounts) it is useful to know that, in most typefaces, figures have a fixed width of one en, so substituting an en space for an absent figure ensures the alignment of the others.

Smaller fixed spaces are used within text to preserve a fixed distance between, for example, initials in names, the dots in an ellipsis, or *pp.* and the number in a page reference. This ensures that the group so spaced will not break at the end of a line. However, since the majority of book texts are now set from authors' word-processor disks, which usually include a variable space or no space at all at these points, this particular form of refinement is becoming rare.

7.15.2 Dashes

Like spaces, dashes come in fixed sizes and have particular functions.

Hyphen (-)

Hyphens link the parts of composite terms (*Romano-British, half-breed*) and compound adjectives (*twentieth-century thinkers, back-lit projection*), and separate parts of words where mispronunciation would otherwise arise (*re-enter, co-operate*). They are also used to avoid ambiguity (*two-year-old dogs, two year-old dogs*). In justified type, they signal the splitting of a word at the end of a line.

En dash (–)

The *en* dash is the width of a lower-case letter *n*. It is used, without spacing, to imply 'to' in a span of numbers or dates (*pp. 33–36, 1939–45*) or to signify opposition or transition (*the England–Ireland match, the Edinburgh–Glasgow road*). With spacing, it can be used as an alternative to the more correct *em* dash as a form of parenthesis (particularly in narrow-column setting, where the width of an em dash may look disruptive).

Em dash (—)

Em dashes are usually used, with variable spaces around them, as a form of parenthesis — denoting a subclause in the same way as a bracket but capable of being used singularly, like a colon, where the subclause ends the sentence.

2-em dash (or two unspaced em dashes) (——)

Used in lists, particularly bibliographies as an alternative to ditto marks (which are rarely used in modern typesetting).

Consult your software manual for the means of accessing these characters. The program which I use on the Macintosh uses *alt–hyphen* for an *en* dash and *alt–shift–hyphen* for an *em* dash.

7.16 DISPLAY

7.16.1 Chapter headings and other part titles

Most books (and journals and magazines) are divided into parts. Usually they are chapters but, in a multi-author work or reference book, they might be articles or subject divisions. In all cases they require marking in such a way that they can easily be found and that they announce the content of the ensuing pages.

Some of the devices available to the designer to signal the start of a chapter are:

- *size*: it is conventional to set display in a larger size.

- *font*: bold or italic versions of the same face as the text — or an entirely different typeface.

- *capitals*: well spaced capitals or small capitals of a larger size.

- *justification*: centred, or even ranged-right, type.

- *vertical spacing*: chapter titles may start lower than the top of the text area (a chapter *drop*) and extra space will usually separate them from the text.

Size

If the format of your book is particularly large and if the nature of the book allows for a degree of flamboyance (e.g. a 'coffee-table' book), you should consider very large type. In other cases, a relatively modest increase in size may be more appropriate. Try twice the text size as a starting point, then

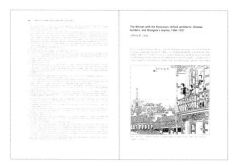

Top left: A simple ranged-left chapter title. The titles are of greatly varying length. The rule provides continuity between chapters, as well as dividing off the author's name.

Twentieth-Century Architecture and its Histories, SAHGB, 2000

Top right: The rule attempts to join an eccentric part title to the chapter title. On other pages, where there is no part title, the rule does not extend beyond the text measure.

Wood Engraving: How to Do it, 2000

Middle left: A very conventional centred chapter title is rescued from dullness by the luxury of space and the aligning picture on the facing page.

Francis Johnson, Architect: a Classical Statement, Oblong, 2001

Left: A restrained, ranged-left title holds its own on this large page partly because of the intrinsic interest of Gill's Joanna typeface. Elsewhere in the book, chapter-opening pages are busier but still seem to work.

The Life and Work of Robert Gibbings, 2003

adjust — remembering that the length of your longest chapter title must be accommodated on the page whilst retaining a reasonable amount of text. (If your design allows part titles a page of their own, or shared with an illustration, your choice of size may be less restricted.)

Font

Some typefaces have an italic font which offers itself as a natural choice for display setting (e.g. Bembo, Palatino). Bold is often less successful, appearing clumsy and overstated (once you have the attention of the reader you should not have to shout). The combination of spacing and typesize with the use of upper and lower-case italic will frequently provide the solution you seek.

A more adventurous solution, though less assured of success, is the use of an entirely different typeface — for instance, Gill Sans combined with text in Sabon. As with colours and tastes, not all pairings are pleasant, and you may need to experiment a little to find out what works for you. One of the ever-present problems with any form of design is that the designer's subjective decisions must strike a chord with the intended audience and only by trial and error can you acquire confidence. Here are a few guidelines to be followed until you feel sure enough to abandon them:

- The less alike the faces are, the better they will probably look together. Try combining serif text face with a sans-serif display face.
- Avoid novelty faces (e.g. Broadway) or faces, such as scripts and black letter (e.g. Marina Script and Old English Text, respectively), which you associate strongly with other printed items such as wedding invitations.
- Typefaces by the same designer often work well in combination — for instance, Eric Gill's Joanna with his Sans face.
- If you favour a display face which does have features in common with your text face, make sure that the size differential discourages comparison. An example might be Palatino italic used with Sabon, where there is some other use of italic in the text.

Capitals

The use of capitals for display is the oldest convention and the most obvious device one can think of. Nevertheless, like all tried and tested solutions, it is often the best. If you use capitals, do not be afraid to letter-space (*track*) them a great deal. If there is a subtitle, or an author's name, try small caps in the same size as the capitals, similarly tracked. Capitals should be larger than the text size but they do not need to be as large as upper- and lower-case display to have an equivalent effect.

Justification

The overall nature of your design may suggest a conventional centred chapter heading or a ranged-left one, or even — for example, in the case of some multi-column designs — a ranged-right one. The important thing is that your design has integrity and that a difference in alignment between the text and the heading does not look arbitrary (e.g. centred display over emphatically asymmetrical text).

Vertical spacing

The convention of dropping chapter headings to align below the head of the text area is not as much followed these days as it was at one time. This is unfortunate because large type needs extra space above as well as below it. On the other hand, your design might derive its impact from strict adherence to a grid and you may not wish to introduce a new, apparently arbitrary, horizontal line. The good thing about using computers to design is that they allow you to experiment — so try out a few options.

What you will certainly find is that you need extra space between the title and the text which starts below it. Unless the *body-size* of the display type is an exact multiple of the body-size of the text, this space will need to vary according to how many lines the title makes. In addition, you may need to vary it to avoid an unsatisfactory break at the bottom of the page. You will need to specify, for your own use, minimum and maximum space to appear below the title. Your page will look odd if the maximum space between title and text is greater than the margin above the title (another reason for considering a dropped title).

7.16.2 Subheadings

Particularly in informational books, subheadings impose a hierarchy on the text and a provide navigational aid to the reader. They should be distinct from the text type, and their size spacing and justification (whether they are centred or ranged left) should announce their level of importance. To avoid varying page depths, it is useful to make the combined depth of the subheading and the space above and below it equal to a multiple of the text *leading* (or body size). The example on the right gives a possible list of five heading levels. By adding other styles, such as capitals with small capitals (*caps and small caps*), and introducing more permutations of size and spacing, more levels can be created.

7.16.3 Preliminary pages

Preliminary pages (*prelims*) contain the title page (the third page), usually a half-title page (the first page), and frequently a contents page (the fifth page) — all of which demand some

AN EXAMPLE OF AN EXTENDED HIERARCHY OF SUBHEADINGS

A. Centred capitals of a type size larger than the text with approximately two lines of space above and one below.

B. Ranged-left capitals of the text size with one and a half lines of space above and half a line below.

C. Ranged-left small capitals with one and a half lines of space above and half a line below.

D. Ranged-left italic upper and lower case with one and a half lines of space above and half a line below.

E. Ranged left italic upper and lower case with one line space above and text running on on the same line after a fixed en space.

use of display. There may also be a frontispiece (the second page, or a separate leaf *tipped in*), which has an effect on design of the title page. Leave the prelims until you have designed the rest of the book: they are the most important pages, requiring longer and deeper consideration, and the familiarity you have acquired with the rest of the book will help you to decide what is needed as well as giving you a structural model for the contents page.

Title page

A title page is something between a welcome and a fanfare. It sets the tone for the whole book and performs the function (which it shares unequally with the cover or jacket) of enticing the casual peruser to venture further into its pages. Your skill as a designer is put to the test here. Try not to go over the top but avoid producing something so understated that it looks like an opportunity entirely missed.

There are rules and principles to help you, particularly if the typography is of a conventional sort but, once you have gained experience of following them, you should consider yourself free to abandon or improve upon them if the needs of the book inspire you to do so.

The text area within which the title-page typography exists may be the same as, or slightly shorter and narrower than that of a normal text page. The words must be arranged to form a cohesive unit and, if this means that the top is dropped, or the base raised from the edge of the text area, then so be it. The margins outside the implicit text area may have similar proportions to those of the text pages (which means in a conventional grid that the centre of the measure will be to the left of the true centre of the page) or it may be decided that, for the half-title and title pages alone, the true, geometric centre will be used. In my experience, the former is to be preferred.

A frontispiece (an illustration or piece of text facing the title page), if one exists, will condition your approach to the title page. Even in the absence of matter facing the title page, you should consider the whole spread as an entity, and there is sometimes an argument for taking the title typography across both pages.

The title page should contain everything a bibliographer or librarian needs to know about the book and nothing else. The title, any subtitle, the author's name, the publisher, and the place and date of publication should usually suffice. There may be other essential information — such as an

Painting
with
Smoke

David
Roberts

Raku
Potter

Lynne Green

Smith Settle • 2000

Four title pages showing different responses to subject matter, page size, and copy:

Top: The squarish page and short title make it possible to confine the type to a narrow ranged-left column leaving room for an illustration. The dedication on the facing page aligns with the top of the pot.

Painting with Smoke, Smith Settle, 2001

FRANCIS
JOHNSON

ARCHITECT

A CLASSICAL STATEMENT

John Martin Robinson
and David Neave

Introduction by
Giles Worsley

Middle: A response to a classical subject. Centred Bembo capitals, letter-spaced, with minimal swelled rules printed in a second colour. Control of type sizes and interlinear spacing creates a strong vase-like silhouette. The type and frontispiece are centred on the text area of the rest of the book.

Francis Johnson, Architect:
A Classical Statement,
Oblong, 2001

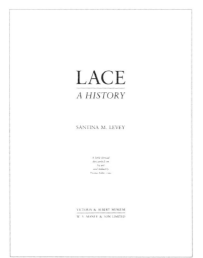

LACE
A HISTORY

SANTINA M. LEVEY

A little thread
declared on
by art
and industry
Thomas Fuller, 1662

VICTORIA & ALBERT MUSEUM
W. S. MANEY & SON LIMITED

Twentieth-Century Architecture
and its Histories

edited by Louise Campbell

SOCIETY OF ARCHITECTURAL HISTORIANS OF GREAT BRITAIN

2000

Below left: Another centred title with a strong silhouette. Here the Sabon type is centred on the page, rather than the text area and the outline is rectangular.

Lace: A History, W. S. Maney
& Son Ltd, 1983

Below right: Ranged-right sans serif combined with a contrasting serif typeface – a theme carried on into the typography of the book.

Twentieth-Century
Architecture and its Histories,
SAHGB, 2000

editor's name, a series title and the volume number in the series — which must be accommodated in your design, but you should discourage editors and authors from adding quotations and dedications — there are proper places for these (see 3.6).

The first choice you will probably face is whether to make your title page symmetrical or asymmetrical. Both in your title-page grid and in your approach to the typography within it you should try to make some reference to the design of the rest of the book and there may be a case for centring the typography if the other pages have a conventional feel, or ranging it left or right if your general design is emphatically asymmetrical. On the other hand, the wording of the title page itself may suggest an approach. A single-word title, for instance, may cry out to be centred on the page whilst a long and complicated text might be less awkward to handle if ranged left.

Symmetrical title pages have a long history and 'rules' have emerged which give the designer a starting point. Some writers have suggested that the area occupied by the type should have the proportions of the human figure — others that it should look like an elegant vase. More helpful, perhaps, is the designer's and printer's concept of *optical centring*. Something which is optically centred lies in a position above true centre. The exact position of the optical centre is a matter of intuition, although I have found that people either agree readily as to where it is or can make no sense whatsoever of the concept. The bulk of the title will conventionally fall on or above the optical centre (the chest of the notional human figure or the widest point of the imagined vase). There is a convention — not necessarily to be observed — that the word *THE*, if it is the first word of the title, stands alone in a smaller size of type (the face of the human figure?). It may help to prepare the reader for the other pages in the book if you can find a vertical position for the title which is echoed in the positioning of the half-title and of the chapter headings, but this may not prove possible. For the same reason, it is often a good idea to align the last line of the title page (the date or place of publication) with the foot of the text area — but remember to conceive the title-page as a unit.

Half-title

Before the middle of the nineteenth century books were sold without bindings (the purchaser being expected have the book bound to his specification as a separate transaction, either with the bookseller or with a bookbinder). The half-title page originally existed to protect the title page from dust whilst on the bookseller's shelf. It carried the title of the book for identification only and provided a convenient leaf for the attachment of endpapers (see 1.5.5) and frontispiece, allowing the title spread to open fully and lie flat.

In more recent times it has become customary for some publishers to use the half-title for series information, a list of books by the same author, or a short biography of the author. In such a case the typography should be in keeping with that of the text pages and its vertical position and margins should echo those of the title page.

If you are designing a traditional half-title page — featuring only the title — the typography should prepare the reader for the title page. This is often done by treating the words in the same way as they are treated on the title page (e.g. centred and letter-spaced capitals) but in miniature. So, if the title page has the title in 48 pt capitals on two lines, the half-title might present the same two lines in 30 pt capitals, *aligned in the same vertical position.*

A half-title page (left), containing only the title of the book, anticipates both the typography and the position of the title on the title page (right).

Engraved Gardens, 2001

Contents page

The contents page is the second most important page in the book. It is not only referred to several times in the course of reading the book but it is often the place to which a prospective reader will come when deciding whether to read the book at all. So it has a function similar to the menus displayed outside restaurants to which diners will come initially to decide at which restaurant they will eat, and then secondly to choose their meal. Like those menus, it needs to be attractive and clear.

Six examples of contents-page layout

Lace: A History, W. S. Maney & Son Ltd, 1983. *Note the listing of illustrations relating to each chapter.*

The Life and Work of Robert Gibbings, 2003

The Life and Works of John Carr of York, Oblong, 2000. *Subheadings, as well as chapter titles, are listed.*

Francis Johnson, Architect: A Classical Statement, Oblong, 2001

Engraved Gardens, 2001

Primrose Hill Press Catalogue, 1999

CONTENTS

		Page	Figures
	Acknowledgements	vii	
	Abbreviations	viii	
	Introduction	1	1 and 2
Chapter I	The Origins of Lace	4	3–12
Chapter II	The Age of Cutwork: c. 1500 to c. 1620	11	13–105
Chapter III	The Triumph of Bobbin Lace: c. 1620 to c. 1675	21	106–182
Chapter IV	Baroque Lace: c. 1650 to c. 1700	31	183–243
Chapter V	The Classic Laces: c. 1660 to c. 1789 Part I: The Laces and their Techniques	43	246–262
Chapter VI	The Classic Laces: c. 1660 to c. 1789 Part II: Fashion and Design	67	263–311
Chapter VII	The Neo-Classical Period: c. 1780 to c. 1815	77	312–360
Chapter VIII	Lace of the Romantic Period: 1816 to 1851	86	370–404
Chapter IX	The Mid-century Lace Boom: 1851 to 1867	98	405–449
Chapter X	Lace in a Period of Instability: 1867 to 1914	106	450–500
	Glossary	110	
	Bibliography	106	
	Index	113	

A contents list should tell the reader what is in the book and where to find it. So, page numbers should be easily associated with the chapter, or other part titles to which they refer. This often means that, rather than arranging them in a column, you can place them at the ends of the titles, perhaps separated by a fixed space (see 7.15.1).

If it is important that the reader understands the range of pages occupied by each chapter, it may be helpful to arrange the page numbers in a column. In such a case, the text measure should be narrowed to bring the numbers closer to the chapter titles. Leader dots (lines of single, double, or treble dots connecting the titles to their respective page numbers) or other linking devices should not be necessary if your layout is effective.

The alignment or indentation of the parts listed should reflect their comparative status. So, if it is considered necessary to list subheadings, they may be indented further than the chapter titles to indicate their place in the hierarchy. Subordinate parts of the book like appendices, indexes, and lists of abbreviations may be similarly distinguished. The use of capitals, small capitals, italics, etc. can also give relative importance to items in the list — whether or not they have been treated in the same way in the text.

Unless there is an overriding reason to the contrary (perhaps arising from the use of an illustration), the title of the contents page should resemble those of the chapters. The use of a narrower measure will cause a ranged-left title to be in a different position, relative to the gutter, from that of the chapter titles, but the typeface and size and its vertical position can, and should, be the same.

The space between the items on the list should be greater than normal line spacing. If the contents list is long enough to extend onto more than one page, its depth on the first page should be the same as the first page of a chapter. If the list is shorter than one page, after the minimum extra space has been added between items, try to space it and position it so that it sits well in the surrounding space, possibly applying the idea of optical centring, especially if you have optically centred the title page.

Title page verso

The reverse side of the title page is not listed above because it does not usually feature display-size type. However, it is important to take it into consideration when designing both the title page and the contents page. The type on this page (usually the fourth page of the prelims, containing copyright information, publishing and printing details, and the *International Standard Book Number*) should be arranged to coincide as much as possible with the position of the type on the title page so that no *show-through* (type visible through the thickness of the paper) will spoil the blank areas of the title-page design. It also needs to balance the type on the contents page. In crude terms, the area of the title page design, truncated at the top and bottom by lines level with the top and bottom of the contents list, is the area you have to work within. This is an ideal not always achievable but worth aspiring to.

7.17 COVER AND DUSTJACKET DESIGN

Regardless of whether the book you are designing will be stocked by bookshops, sold by direct mail, or distributed free of charge, the first function of the cover or jacket is to entice the reader into the book. Its other purposes are to inform and to protect. In a successful design these three objectives must be achieved with equal success. There is no conflict in this aim unless you introduce it yourself by deciding that the only attractive design is one which fails to communicate the title of the book, or that your sense of aesthetics obliges you to use materials which will not withstand normal handling.

7.17.1 *Materials and economy*

In a chapter on typography we need not explore the question of materials in any great depth (see 2). It is sufficient to note that covers and jackets can be printed on to a wide range of papers and boards: some of them coated (art and matt-art papers and boards), some of them tinted (cartridges, and coated papers), and some of them textured (embossed and naturally rough papers, often called cartridges). Appropriate weights for a jacket range from about 130 gsm to 150 gsm, and those for a cover from around 250 gsm to 300 gsm.

The economics of the project will be one influence on your decision regarding the number of colours you can afford to work with. It is normal to design covers and jackets in any one of a range of differently costed options from tinted paper printed in one colour to matt art paper, printed in more than the four process colours and laminated to produce a resilient matt or glossy surface.

The inclusion of a picture, if available, will affect the cost and your choice of material. Art and matt art papers provide a better surface than uncoated and tinted papers for the printing of colour and tone images, whilst uncoated papers are ideal for line images like wood engravings.

7.17.2 Design

The essential elements in a jacket or cover design must be taken in at a glance. If your design takes too long to convey its message, the prospective reader's eye will have moved on and your chance will have been lost. Integrating the type with the image is one way of furthering this aim. Another is to go for clarity, confining the text on the front of the book to the title and the author, using large sizes of a legible typeface (as with title

The dotted lines on the illustrations below and on the next page indicate the edges of the front of the book.

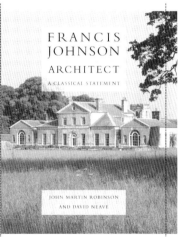

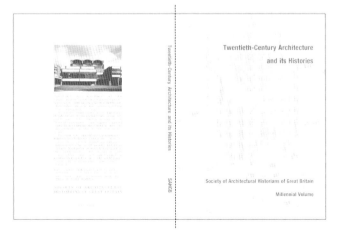

Above: A dustjacket which accommodates wordy text by overlaying it on a lightened panel (see 6.8.1)

Francis Johnson, Architect: A Classical Statement, Oblong, 2001

Left: The ranged-right type on this cover echoes the design of the title page

Twentieth-Century Architecture and its Histories, SAHGB, 2000

The vertical rectangle which accommodates the text and picture on the front of this simple cover is reflected in the design of the back. The subdued tone of the title panel and author's name adds emphasis to the black image.

Engraved Gardens, 2001

pages, avoid novelty or non-bookish typefaces) and taking care with the positioning and spacing of the letters.

Utilizing the typefaces used in the book and echoing the design of the title page promote a pleasing unity — but, if you can see a better way of combining impact with communication which involves introducing an entirely new set of fonts, you should go for it. Commercial publishers, particularly of fiction, abandoned the idea of unifying the inside and outside of the book years ago yet still produce many strikingly designed books.

The cover or jacket is not a page of the book. You do not have to reflect the margins of the text pages, since these were devised to work for a double-page spread, and anything centred horizontally should be in the true centre of the book (although the principle of optical vertical centring still applies). Analysis of cover designs on my own bookshelves suggests that many designers consider the top, right-hand quarter of a jacket or cover to have special significance for the placing of type in asymmetrical designs. A contemporary trend in this respect is the centring of the title and author to form a symmetrical unit then the placing of that unit in an asymmetrical position.

The spine should give the title, the author, and the publisher (or publisher's logo) and should read from top to bottom, unless the book is in a series which has the type going the other way. The reason for this is that it remains legible when the book is lying face-up on a flat surface.

The back of a paperback cover should contain a description of the book (*blurb*), possibly a brief biography of the author, the *ISBN*, and the price. The back of a dustjacket may also contain all this information, although it is conventional for the blurb about book and author to appear on the jacket flaps (the ends which fold inside the book's hard cover). You may wish to use the back of the jacket for a second picture or to introduce some text about the publisher or series of publications, if there is one.

Colour

If your budget allows for colour, this may be the only opportunity you have to combine colour with typography. There can be no rules to help you in this, but here are a few pointers:

- Consider using an all-over solid colour covering all parts of the cover or jacket which is not occupied by a picture, then set the type in black or white to contrast with the background colour. The colour can be printed as a separate fifth colour or made up out of the four process colours.

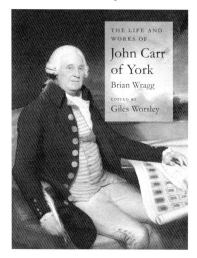

The top right-hand corner of this colour cover picture provides the ideal location for the title. Although it is reproduced here in black and white, a dark red sampled from it was used for the spine and back. Note that the text appears on a lightened panel in which the image can still be seen (see 6.8.1).

The Life and Works of John Carr of York, Oblong, 2000

- Choose, for the background colour or for coloured type, a colour which appears in any picture you are using.

- Alternatively, choose a colour which appears to contrast with the dominant colours in the picture.

- If there is no picture, try to use simple colours with a hint of sophistication (like dark red, cobalt, mustard yellow, dark green, etc.) or primary colours, rather than complex colours which would be very difficult to mix if they were paints and are equally difficult to describe. Simple colours are memorable and do not detract so readily from the appeal of the typographical design.

- Some colours have associations for people (however politically incorrect they may sound when described). For instance, you might wish to avoid pinks and violets when designing a book celebrating Rugby Union, or grey and khaki for a book on confectionery. I was told as a novice designer working in London that some Middle-Eastern cultures attach negative associations to the colour orange and I have not subsequently encountered any reason to doubt it.

Book typography is a large subject, occupying the best part of many books on general typography, having a longer history than any other form of graphic design, and being still the most difficult aspect of book design for the layman to grasp. This book attempts only to provide a basis for acquiring skills and knowledge. Most experienced typographers look critically at every bit of printed type they see and read eagerly each article and book on the subject which comes their way.

8 equipment and method

8.1 INTRODUCTION

This book was written on a laptop PC using Microsoft Word and designed on an Apple Macintosh using QuarkXPress. Most of the writing was done on a kitchen table and the designing was done on an office desk equipped with a typist's chair. This does not tell the whole story but it illustrates the increasingly moveable nature of a job which used to require something resembling a technical drawing office. When one tries to define which computer is right for a particular task and what peripherals (printers, scanners, etc.) are needed, one runs into such a wealth of choice and so many contradictory opinions that it becomes necessary to generalize. The following generalizations are intended to point the reader in the right direction and equip him or her with the right questions to ask.

8.2 PCS AND MACS

PC stands for 'personal computer'. However, the term is usually used to mean a computer using a Microsoft operating system (MSDOS, or Windows). At one time such a computer would have been called an IBM clone, but it is so long since IBM's computers were everyone's first thought, and so many other manufacturers have now become household names, that the term is no longer used. PCs were once favoured by accountants and managers because of their perceived number-crunching superiority and considered less capable than the Apple Macintosh when it came to graphic applications. Today, the principal hurdle facing the European designer using a PC is industry prejudice. In the USA, PCs have always shared the graphics market with Macs.

The Mac is still the favoured computer in design studios, printing firms, and repro houses in the UK. Because we tend to replace old equipment with equivalent new equipment, and because the original reasons for preferring one type of computer over the other (price in the case of PCs and the graphic superiority of Macs) have largely disappeared, this bias is likely to continue for some time to come. Since around the year 2000, Macintoshes and PCs have been able to use the same peripherals, which means that, if you use a Mac, you no longer need to invest in expensive SCSI printers and scanners. There are Mac clones just as there were once IBM clones.

The result of the development of both types of computer is that the specification of the equipment (size of memory, speed of processor, etc.) is more important than whether it is a Mac or a PC.

If you are likely to be designing for a limited number of printing firms, or you are part of an organization which already uses computers for graphic applications, check their preferences before committing yourself.

8.3 WORD PROCESSORS

I do not intend to advocate the use of word-processing software for book design. It was not designed for that purpose and should not in truth be used for it. However, designers using *dtp* (*desktop-publishing*) software will often need the help of a word-processing program to convert text on an author's disk into something which the dtp software can use. Also, word processors provide an easy means of keying large amounts of text on the (increasingly rare) occasions when that proves necessary.

If you *are* a word-processor operator and you have been asked to design a book without the aid of desktop-publishing software, you will still find the principles explained in this book helpful.

For converting and editing authors' text the most useful word-processor software currently available must be Word, if only because most authors have it. If we did not consider this a good reason, we could argue that Corel WordPerfect is better because of its superior 'reveal codes' option and because of the ease with which you can program buttons to produce your own codes and text. In fact, either of these programs will serve admirably for the designer's needs. Make sure you have the latest version and install all the 'filters' which enable the software to read files from other word-processing programs.

To run word-processing software adequately, you need a PC or a Mac with at least 64 Mb (megabytes) of *RAM* (*random access memory*) and a hard disk of at least 4 gigabytes (1 Gb = 1000 Mb). It is wise to buy the fastest processor you can afford, since processors are being developed at such a rate that anything you buy will be obsolescent almost before you open the box and companies will eventually stop writing software for it. At the time of writing this book, 700 MHz processors were considered normal: by the time it went to press anything under 1.7 GHz (1700 MHz) was said to be incapable of running the latest software. A 15″ screen may be big enough for you: have a good look at one and decide whether the extra cost of a 17″ or 19″ monitor might be justified in your case. Increasingly, in any case, systems are being supplied with bigger monitors.

Note that if you plan to use the same computer to run dtp software, the specification will be higher than that needed for word processing.

The only other equipment you need is a printer. For word processing, a laser printer which produces black print quickly is sufficient. There are many manufacturers of laser printers. When buying, check the cost of replacement cartridges and the number of A4 pages which each cartridge is meant to produce.

8.4 DESKTOP PUBLISHING

8.4.1 Hardware

See 8.2 for a brief discussion of PCs and Macs.

The major desktop-publishing programs have been written for both PCs and Macs and there is an increasing degree of common file-handling between them. If all users of PCs and Macs running the same program could count on complete compatibility, there would be no need to advocate the use of one type of computer or the other. However, this not yet the case and, in the UK at least, there is still a strong bias towards using Macs for design and print. This being so, the ideal first machine for the prospective book designer must still be an Apple Macintosh with at least 256 Mb of RAM, a large hard disk, a fast processor, a good graphics card (though it need not have the 3-D power of a 'gaming' card), and a 21″ monitor. To this should be attached a desktop scanner with true 1200 *dpi* (*dots per inch*) resolution or better and a transparency hood, a Post-Script colour printer, and a drive capable of recording large files on removable media (for example, writeable compact disks — CD-Rs).

There is a difference between true, optical resolution and the greater, software-enhanced resolution claimed by most scanners. See 8.4.3.

A PC with a similar specification will do just as well if you have established that the printers and repro houses with whom you are likely to work will accept PC files.

8.4.2 Software

There are currently two programs competing for supremacy, QuarkXPress and PageMaker. Of these two, there is a bias in the world of design and print towards Quark (which is probably more a matter of custom than continuous reassessment) although there are designers who swear by PageMaker. There are other programs which will enable you to design and produce a book, some of them considerably cheaper than the main two, but you should ask around to see whether printers you are likely to use can accept their files before deciding to use them.

To make yourself fully capable of designing books on your computer you will also need a photo-editing program like PhotoShop or PaintShop, and (less essential but very useful) a drawing program like Illustrator or Freehand.

8.4.3 Peripherals

Printers

Ideally, every designer would have a laser printer for black-only output with a high level of accuracy, and an inkjet printer with which to proof colour work. Inkjet printers produce a less well defined image but they are cheaper than laser printers and bridge the gap between black-and-white proofs and professional colour proofs.

If colour proofs which are more representative of the final printed image are needed, there are two types: those which are produced from your dtp files (really high-quality inkjet proofs), and those which are made from film output. The second type is very expensive (because of the need to produce film first) and should be offered only as a final check before printing. Unless you are spending the sort of budget which you would need to set up a repro department, you should leave both types to the printer or repro company.

You can get away with only buying an inkjet printer, particularly if you are planning to offer someone else's professional colour proofs at the final stage, but you should ensure that it is a PostScript printer and that the driver on your computer is a PostScript driver. Beware of phrases like 'PostScript emulation' or 'PostScript enabled'.

Scanners

Scanners are remarkably cheap considering what they do, and it is well worth buying one of the slightly more expensive ones if it offers true, optical 1200 dpi resolution both horizontally

As with computers, the standard specifications of peripherals, such as scanners and printers, are constantly improving. So, if you are reading this book more than a few months after its publication, you may find that higher resolutions have become commonplace.

and vertically. Most scanners scan at their highest true resolution then use software to produce an image of a higher resolution (e.g. 9600 dpi). If you are scanning at a nominal 2400 dpi on a 1200 dpi scanner, the software is calculating the likely colour values which fall between the points which it can actually see. This normally produces a perfectly acceptable result and, for simple line images, you can even make repro-standard scans on a 1200 dpi desktop scanner. On the other hand, a nominal 2400 dpi scan from a 600 dpi scanner would not be likely to prove adequate.

Disk writers

There are so many media for storing and transporting computer files that it is impossible to make a single recommendation. If you know which printing company or repro house you are likely to be using, ask them what they use. Zip disks are fairly common but most people have the kind which is limited to 100 Mb (too little for most books, particularly if they are illustrated). Compact-disk writers are a good bet because they allow over 600 Mb of storage and almost everyone has a CD drive. If you buy a drive for rewriteable CDs you can use it for backing up the data on your computer — but the CDs you produce may not be accepted by all other computers.

See 8.6 for a list of reference material and instruments which you will need in addition to your computer and its peripherals.

8.5 DESIGNING WITHOUT A COMPUTER

There is still a place for the designer without a computer. In fact, many of the books on graphic design and typography currently in print fail to acknowledge the change which computers have brought about and give excellent advice for the designer who proposes to remain in the pre-computer world.

For a full description of the equipment needed by the committed pencil-and-paper designer see *The Thames and Hudson Manual of Typography* (Ruari McLean, 1980) — the book itself is good example of practical book design and offers much other information which you will find useful. It is possible to design a book at a dining-room table or office desk, with only a layout pad, a typescale, a pencil, a setsquare, and typeface reference material but, however well you equip yourself, today you are giving instructions to a person with a computer. You must decide whether, in terms of job-satisfaction as well as economy, it is better to employ a chauffeur or to drive the car yourself.

8.6 REFERENCE MATERIAL AND INSTRUMENTS

Whether or not you are using a computer, there are certain simple items of equipment which you cannot do without:

8.6.1 Typescale

A steel ruler which has 12 pt and 10 pt ems marked along its edges as well as inches and/or centimetres. You need this for measuring text width. It also provides a good edge along which to cut with a scalpel or to draw with a pencil.

8.6.2 Depth scale

A plastic ruler with wide slits in it, giving it several edges which are marked off in different point measurements. Used to establish the body size of type, to quickly measure the number of lines of type on a page, and to mark off depths when working with a pencil or drawing pen.

8.6.3 24-inch ruler

For measuring or drawing lines longer than your typescale. Try to find one with a raised drawing edge if you propose to draw with a pen. Mine has a steel strip along one edge which I use as a guide for cutting.

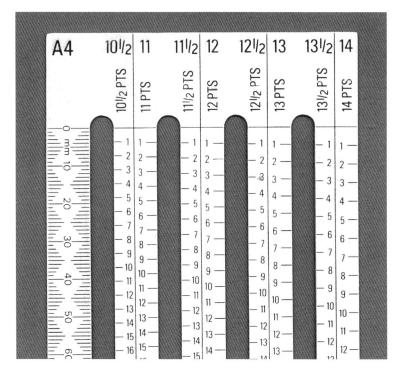

Depth scale (detail shown full size)

8.6.4 Scalpel

Used principally for cutting proofs to size, also for sharpening pencils. A small craft knife is an alternative, but a metal Swann-Morton surgical scalpel, equipped with straight-edged non-sterilized blades, is the optimum choice.

8.6.5 Pens

Although I gave up using a technical drawing pen when I started designing on a computer, I still use pens of several types and colours. Overhead-projector pens are needed for marking up the backs of some photographs and for marking corrections on film and non-porous types of proof. Ordinary roller-ball or fibre-tip pens are needed for marking corrections on paper proofs and writing messages to clients and suppliers. Occasionally, I find I need a fine black pen to draw a character in order to clarify a point with a client — a drawing pen would still have a use here, but a good roller-ball pen suffices.

8.6.6 Pencils

A soft pencil (2B–4B) is the best implement for writing on the back of artwork. If you must make marks on the front which a camera or scanner will not pick up, you need a very light blue coloured pencil — but marking the front of artwork should be avoided wherever possible.

8.6.7 Adhesives

Used mainly for producing mock-ups (proofs cut and pasted to look like the finished article) and composite artwork, a can of spray mount adhesive and a Pritt Stick are indispensable. You can also buy spray adhesive which remains tacky, allowing you to reposition artwork several times.

8.6.8 Typeface reference material

Suppliers' catalogues enable you to discuss typefaces with client, author, or editor, and to make your own decisions about which type to use. Tracing sheets, if you can get them, are even better because they show the type in different sizes.

8.6.9 Lightbox

Not strictly an essential unless you are working with a lot of transparencies, a modest-sized (e.g. A3) lightbox can be a great help when discussing illustrations and checking film.

8.7 PROCEDURE

This book does not set out to teach you how to use your software. The manuals which came with it, supplemented by any books which you can find about it (these are often useful because they tell you the things which the writers of the manual have missed out) and any help you can get from friends and colleagues, should bring you to the point where this book takes over. The aim of this book is to introduce the concepts with which a book designer using that software should be familiar. The circumstances affecting each book are different and may require a degree of improvisation, but the following gives you some idea of what to expect to happen and in what order:

8.7.1 Agreeing the design

Your 'client' may be a publisher, an editor, an author, or someone else (even, perhaps, yourself), but it is likely that before starting in earnest you will need to demonstrate one or more approaches to the design. It is always best, if possible, to use the actual text and pictures which will appear in the book. Typically, you may need to proof a couple of double-page spreads and the cover or dust-jacket in one or more designs. A good colour-inkjet printer is ideal for this. It is worth cutting these first proofs to size and scoring them so that they resemble real pages from the book: it avoids misunderstanding and expedites agreement. Save the files and name them carefully so that you can use the right one as a template later.

It is a good idea to tackle some of the more problematical parts of the book in these *specimen pages*. Otherwise, your agreed design may prove inadequate to its task when you come to design the whole book.

Beware of offering too many choices. Many people will feel the need to express their awareness of design by asking you to combine elements of two or more of your initial designs. It is a practice to be argued against. And you would not be well advised to submit what appears to you to be an obviously inferior design to weight the client's judgement in favour of your self-evidently superior one — they almost always go for the dummy.

8.7.2 Designing the book

This is the largest part of the work. You will probably receive the author's text on disk. If not, you must key it, have someone

See 11 for a checklist of the questions to answer and stages to complete when designing a book.

else key it, or use *OCR* (*optical character recognition*) software (which often comes free with scanners). In any case, you will end up with a text file in a word-processor's native format, *RTF* (*rich-text format* — which preserves some basic formatting such as italic), or simple text. You will quickly find out which of these your dtp software accepts most readily. Check any new keying or OCR reading for errors or print it out and have it read against the original copy by another person.

If you are lucky, the author will not have attempted to scan the pictures in advance. It is better to have control over this part of the process. If your design is a simple one (e.g. text with the occasional text-width picture) you can size the pictures (see 6.5–6.7) and have them scanned by the printer or repro house before you start. Alternatively, you can produce positional scans (see 6.2) at a low resolution (e.g. 150 dpi for greyscale and colour, and 500 dpi for line), design your book, and then use the result to size the originals for substitution at the output stage.

With pictures and text ready in a useable form you must now design your pages a spread at a time. Do not expect this to be done in less than 10 to 20 minutes a page, depending on the complexity of the design. Consult your software manual about the use of *styles*. These are formats which you can apply to paragraphs of raw text. They speed the process up and ensure consistency between sections of the book. You will find that they can be extracted from the pages of the agreed design quite easily. Note, however, that if (as you sometimes must) you strip out all the formatting in your raw text before applying a style, you will need to reinstate the italic type manually.

If you have a large amount of text from which you need to take sections individually and place them in your grid, it helps to flow the text into an interim version of the book, which has the right text measure but lacks pictures, running heads, etc. Apply all your formatting to this relatively simple text-only file, save it, then lift out the text a section at a time to paste into your grid. This method is particularly useful if your formatting of the text involves any 'searching-and-replacing' (e.g. replacing *lining* with *old-style* figures) because the whole book can be searched at one go.

8.7.3 Proofing

When the design is ready you must proof it for the editor, author, etc. to read, check, and amend. Each person who is going to read the proofs will need their own set. The person who is taking overall responsibility for the proofs will need an extra one so that they can return one to you and keep one for reference. If the design was approved on the basis of mock-up spreads trimmed to size and scored, you should not need to trim the proofs or present them as spreads. If there is a great deal of colour in the book, you should produce one set on a colour inkjet printer — black-and-white may be acceptable for the rest. Black-and-white proofs can be produced more quickly on your laser printer or, if you have access to a photocopier, photocopied from your inkjet proofs. Make sure that any errors or adjustments which you spot after proofing are marked on every set of proofs.

Send the proofs, together with the author's text, but not the originals of the illustrations, to the person who has taken responsibility for returning the proofs to you, unless you have been asked to send proofs directly to more than one person.

When the proofs are returned to you they will have some alterations marked on them (if there are no such corrections, it is likely that the editor has not read them properly). Corrections arising from errors in your work (e.g. italic words which have become roman in the course of your application of styles) are your responsibility. Conventionally, alterations arising from errors in the author's or editor's work and new copy inserted at the proof stage are called *authors' corrections* and are charged to the publisher. It is advisable to draw attention to this possible source of extra cost at the outset — otherwise you may be accused of misrepresenting your charges.

For a complete list of proof-correction marks, see *MHRA Style Book* (MHRA, 1996) or *BS5261: Guide to Copy Preparation and Proof Correction* (British Standards Institution, 1976).

After correction, it is a good idea to submit a second proof, together with the editor's returned first proof, so that your correcting of the first proof can be checked. It should be politely pointed out that this is not an opportunity to make further alterations to the text.

At the same time, show the printer (or binder, if you are dealing with him separately) a proof of the cover or dustjacket so that the width of the *spine* can be checked. You will probably have arrived at this by measuring a book with similar paper and the same number of pages. The binder should make up a dummy of the book, using the correct paper, and can advise you of any alteration you must make to the spine.

8.7.4 Output

When all proofing and correcting has been done, and everyone is happy with the result, it only remains for you to supply a file, or files, to the printer (or repro company) which can be used to output film.

Because of the way they work, some printers require bromide paper or laser output on paper. Both systems entail a drop in quality — the second more so than the first — and are to be discouraged. It may, however, be a matter of agreement between the printer and the publisher and, thus, out of your hands. I would always make the opportunity to let the publisher know the implications of the option he or she has taken.

The files you supply may already be complete with final scans. If not, the person to whom you supply it needs to know that it is their job to substitute final scans for your positionals. To do this they will need fully marked-up originals (see 6.7).

Your files may be in the default format of your software, PostScript files with embedded fonts, or *PDF* files. Your software manual will show you how to produce various forms of file. If your printer does not insist on a PostScript or PDF file, it is probably best not to supply one. PostScript files cannot be corrected, and any errors which are discovered after you part company with the file will entail your making a replacement file. If you supply your software's default (or native) files make sure that the person who will output them has the same version of the same fonts as you have used. (It is currently illegal to simply copy the fonts with your files and supply them to another party.)

8.7.5 Checking film and outturn sheets

Your responsibility may end with the submission of files for output. On the other hand, you may have been asked by the publisher to *see the book through the press*. It is helpful, in this case, to be given the opportunity to see either the film or a proof taken from it before the plates are made (see 1.3). *Ozalids* (which provide a negative image if the printer is using negative film) are a common medium for proofing film but do not show colour. *Cromalins* are an expensive form of pre-press colour proofing. If the plates are being exposed directly from your dtp files (see 1.3.1), there are comparatively low-cost, electronically generated proofs which perform the same function.

You should then either approve the printed sheets as they come off the printing machine (*pass them on press*) or be sent *outturn sheets* (rolled or roughly folded printed sheets) for approval. Printers often discourage the passing of sheets on press because it leads to very expensive machinery standing idle whilst their customer deliberates about what may appear to be inconsequential aspects of the printing. On the other hand, they must accept that anything found wrong with the outturn sheet may entail a complete reprint of that sheet at their expense. Whatever you do, do not make changes of your own at this stage — the cost of reprinting will be your responsibility.

9 note on editorial style

MOST COMMERCIAL and academic society publishers have a *house style*. This may be a simple matter of preferring UK to US spelling, or recommending a list of abbreviations for journal titles, or it may be a lengthy document giving rules for every aspect of a publication. These rules can prescribe such things as the form of references, the treatment of quotations, the use of italics, abbreviations, capitalization, punctuation, and spelling.

Consistency in all these things is to be desired, although the acceptance of this idea depends on a shared perception of common sense, and it is a hard concept to justify to the unconvinced. The absence of consistency in matters of editorial style can be thought indicative of a lack of thoroughness in other aspects of the work, casting doubt on the author's integrity and the publisher's professionalism.

A definition of the designer's role is not likely to include the imposition of editorial style, still less the creation of a house style, but I have often found in practice that it does.

The items most commonly affected by decisions regarding editorial style are:

- the treatment of bibliographical references: the order of items; in what circumstances *p.* proceeds a page number; arabic or roman numerals for volume numbers; the position of authors' initials for first-named and subsequent authors; the means of distinguishing between article, publication, and series titles; etc.
- the treatment of inclusive numbers: *145–148*, *145–48*, or *145–8*.
- whether or not there is a full point after *Dr*, *St*, *Rd*, etc.
- whether *–ise* and *–isation* or *–ize* and *–ization* word endings.
- the italicization (or otherwise) and punctuation of common Latin-derived words and abbreviations like *et al.*, *ibid.*, *op. cit.*, etc.

See 10 for recommended further reading on editorial style.

10 further reading

THIS IS A SHORT LIST compiled in part from books on my bookshelf, some of them referred to in the writing of this book, and in part from the memory of books once owned. Some of the titles listed are out of print. For more extensive lists on specific subjects, refer to the bibliographies of the books here listed.

Book design

Hendel, Richard, *On Book Design* (New Haven and London: Yale University Press, 1998)

Hochuli, Jost and Kinross, Robin, *Designing Books: Practice and Theory* (London: Hyphen Press, 1996)

Martin, Douglas, *An Outline of Book Design* (London: Blueprint/Publishers Association, 1989)

Williamson, Huw, *Methods of Book Design: The Practice of an Industrial Craft*, 3rd edn (New Haven and London: Yale University Press, 1983)

Copy preparation, editorial style, hyphenation, and proof correction

Butcher, Judith, *Copy-Editing: The Cambridge Handbook for Editors, Authors, and Publishers*, 3rd edn (Cambridge: Cambridge University Press, 1992)

BS 5261: *Guide to Copy Preparation and Proof Correction*, parts 1 and 2 (London: British Standards Institution, 1975 and 1976)

Collins Gem Dictionary of English Spelling (London: Harper Collins, 1993)

MHRA Style Book: Notes for Authors, Editors, and Writers of Theses, 5th edn (London: Modern Humanities Research Association, 1996)

Paper

Paper, its Making, Merchanting and Usage. The Paper Merchants Text Book, rev. edn (London: National Association of Paper Merchants, 1978)

Typography

Baines, Phil and Halsham, Andrew, *Type and Typography* (London: Laurence King, 2002)

Lewis, John, *Typography: Basic Principles* (London: Studio Vista, 2nd edn, 1967)

McLean, Ruari, *The Thames and Hudson Manual of Typography* (London: Thames & Hudson, 1980)

Tschichold, Jan, *Asymmetric Typography* (London: Faber & Faber, 1967) (transl. By Ruari McLean from *Typographische Gestaltung*, Basle, 1935)

11 checklist

THIS LIST DESCRIBES the stages to go through and the questions to ask for a straightforward design project. The order in which you find you need to tackle some of the items listed may differ from this list and, in any case, some of them must be considered simultaneously. It may help you to photocopy these two pages and fill the boxes in as you go along.

1   Is there a budget for the production of this book? (State how much.)

2   Has a specific number of pages been requested? (State how many.)   See 1.5.1 and 4.2.

3   Is the book to be hardback, paperback, or both?   See 1.5.

4   What is your chosen page size?   x   See 4.

    Is it suitable for the required pictures and text?   See 5.5.

    Will it come out of an available sheet size without unnecessary wastage?   See 4.2–4.7.

    Have you considered its effect on the length of the book?

5   Decide text and picture grids.   See 4.8 and 5.

    Are the resulting text measure and margins suitable for sustained reading (if appropriate)?   See 5.5 and 7.12.

    Have you incorporated sufficient flexibility for handling the illustrations?   See 5.5.

    Have you considered the effect of your grid on the length of the book?

6   Is 4-colour printing to be used?   See 1.3.2 and 1.4.1.

    If so, throughout the book ... ?

    ... or part? (Describe colour use.)

7   Is there a requirement for a 'spot' colour? (State colour if known.)   See 1.4.2.

8   What typeface(s) are you using? (State use of each — e.g. *captions*.)   See 7.1–7.10.

    Is your main text typeface sufficiently legible?   See 7.10.3.

    Does it appear to you to be appropriate for the subject?

See 7.11 and 7.16.1.	9	What type sizes? (State use.)	☐
			☐
			☐
		Are these sizes sufficiently legible for their purpose?	☐
		Have you considered their effect on the length of the book?	☐
	10	Set up the above parameters in your dtp software.	☐
See 2.1–2.3.	11	What weight and type of paper is to be used …	
		… for the text?	☐
		… for the cover?	☐
		… for the dustjacket?	☐
		… for any other purpose (e.g. endpapers)?	☐
See 8.7.2.	12	Is the text in a form suitable for importing into your pages?	☐
	13	If not, convert it in your word-processing software.	☐
See 8.7.2.	14	Are the pictures in a form suitable for importing into your pages?	☐
		If not, convert them in your picture-editing software …	☐
See 1.2, 6.4–6.7, and 8.7.2.		… or, if they have been supplied as artwork, have them scanned.	☐
See 8.7.1.	15	Have you agreed to supply specimen pages?	☐
		If so, import sufficient text and pictures to fill about four representative pages and lay them out.	☐
See 8.7.2.	16	You are ready to design the book.	☐
		Keep your files to handleable sizes (e.g. a chapter each).	☐
		Make sure that your page-numbering is sequential between files.	☐
See 7.17.		Don't forget to design the dustjacket/cover and other peripheral items such as printed endpapers and spine blocking.	☐
	17	Proof the whole book and check the proofs yourself.	☐
See 8.7.3.	18	If satisfied, prepare proofs for the editor or author.	☐
		How many sets of proofs are needed?	☐
		Remember to send the original hard-copy typescript (if there was one) with the proofs, but not usually the pictures.	☐
	19	On return of the proofs, make all corrections then proof again.	☐
See 8.7.4.	20	On return of the final proofs, correct and supply files to the printer.	☐
See 8.7.5.	21	If you have undertaken to do so, inspect the film — or pre-press proofs — and arrange to visit the printer to check the first printed sheets as they come off the press.	☐

12 glossary

A3	paper size, 420 x 297 mm.
A4	page or paper size, 297 x 210 mm.
A5	page or paper size, 210 x 148 mm.
arabic figures	the numerals we all use (1, 2, 3, 4), as opposed to *roman numerals* (I, II, III, IV).
art paper	paper with a thick coating which gives it its texture. Particularly suitable for printing colour and *half-tone* images, art paper may have a gloss, silk, or matt surface. This book is printed on a matt art paper.
ascender	part of a *lower-case* letter which extends above the *x-height*.
assembly	arranging and fixing film pages, or *imposed* groups of pages, ready for printing down onto a *litho* plate.
authors' corrections	corrections to a proof which do not arise from errors on the part of the designer or printer. The cost of making these corrections is usually born by the publisher or the author.
B1	paper size, 720 x 1020 mm.
B2	paper size, 720 x 520 mm (or, from some manufacturers, 710 x 520 mm).
back margin	see *margins*.
baseline	the line upon which most characters appear to sit and below which *descenders* descend.
binding (book binding)	collating the pages of a book and securing them to form a unit – usually also attaching a *cover* or *case* for the protection of the pages.
bleed	(1) extend (picture or area of colour) beyond the edge of a page so that it will reach the edge when trimmed; (2) the 3 mm margin necessary to do this.
blocking	on the spine or front of a cased book (sometimes also on paperback covers or dustjackets), foil applied with a combination of heat and pressure so that the design is impressed into the surface of the case. *Gold blocking* uses metallic, gold-coloured foil: *blind blocking* produces the impressed design without foil.
blurb	common term for text used on covers, jackets, and advertising leaflets to promote or describe a book or its author.
body size	the body size of type is equivalent, in current parlance, to the *leading* and not to the nominal size. So, 10 on 12 point Times has a body size of 12 *points*.

bold	type of a heavier weight than *roman*. Used in *display* and, occasionally, in informational typography to highlight numbered paragraphs or to identify subjects under discussion. Excessive use of bold type can be disruptive and ugly and should be avoided. **This is bold.**
book binding	see *binding*.
book block (sewn middle)	a book before it is covered or *case-bound*. Thus, all the *sections* gathered and either *sewn* and *endpapered* for *sewn binding* or with backs cut off for *perfect binding*.
book designer	the deviser and specifier of the physical form of a book. A book designer should include typography amongst his skills. See *typographer*, *compositor*.
bulk	the thickness of a book between the boards of the case or cover (and thus excluding them). Also used to mean the thickness of paper relative to its weight (so a 'bulky book wove' is one which has great thickness and comparatively little weight).
calender	give a smooth surface to paper by passing it between rollers either during (calendering) or after (super calendering) the paper-making process.
cap height	the height of a capital I in a given size and typeface.
cartridge papers	strong, rough-surfaced papers, traditionally used to make cartridges for shotguns. Today used for lithographic printing (because of their dimensional stability) and drawing (because of their rough surface). See *coated cartridge papers*.
case binding (hardback binding)	binding in heavy boards covered in cloth or a cloth substitute. The spine of a cased book, which is not glued directly to the pages, may be either flat (square) or rounded. Traditionally, the first and last pages of the book are attached to the boards with *endpapers*.
centre	centred type is positioned equidistant from the edges of the *text measure* or page. Type may also be said to be vertically centred on the page or on the text depth. See *optical centring*.
chapter drop	distance below the top of the text area at which chapter titles and other similar display headings are aligned in traditional book typography.
Cicero (Didot)	The continental European standard of type measurement. See *Pica*.
coated cartridge papers	*cartridge papers* to which a china-clay coating has been applied to make them suitable for *halftone* and colour printing. Coated cartridges are lightly *calendered* to give them a smooth but not glossy surface.
collate	collect the parts of a book in the right order, ready for *sewing*, *perfect binding*, or *wire-stitching*. May involve insetting parts of *sections* as well as simply *gathering* sections.
compositor	craftsman who sets and corrects text using metal type. At one time, the term was also used for operators of electronic typesetting equipment but this use of it does not appear to have survived. See *book designer*, *typographer*.

cover	the outer part of a paperback book. Usually of a heavier, more durable material than the pages. Protects and advertises the book. See *dustjacket*.
Cromalin	a type of colour proof which can be produced from positive film before printing plates are made.
cropping (masking)	removing the edges of a picture to reveal the part which is meant to print.
Crown (Metric Crown)	paper size, 384 x 504 mm. *Double Crown* is 504 x 768 mm.
Crown Quarto	page size, 246 x 189 mm.
cut-out	a picture with the background removed, leaving the subject confined to its own outline.
dashes	Dashes of different sizes have different functions:
	hyphen connecting compound nouns and adjectives (amino-acids, copper-plated).
	en dash UNSPACED to imply transition or opposition (1934–45, the Iran–Iraq conflict, the London–Brighton road).
	SPACED – in some modern typography – as an alternative to parentheses or singly in place of a colon or semicolon.
	em dash SPACED — traditionally — as an alternative to parentheses, or a colon or semicolon when used to separate clauses in a sentence; also, in lists, as an alternative to ditto marks.
	double-em dash (——) in lists, as an alternative to ditto marks.
Demy (Metric Demy)	paper size, 444 x 564 mm. *Quad Demy* is 888 x 1128 mm.
Demy Octavo	page size, 216 x 138 mm.
densitometer	an electronic instrument for measuring the density of black or coloured ink.
depthscale	instrument for measuring the depth of text in lines of the typesize. The common design gives units from 6 pt to 14 pt in half-point increments.
descender	part of a *lower-case* letter which extends below the baseline.
display	type of a larger size than the text, used for chapter titles, headings, *title page*, *half-title*, etc.
Didot	see *Cicero*.
Double Crown	see *Crown*.
dpi	dots per inch, the measure of *resolution* of a scanner or a desk-top printer.
drawn-on	of book covers, wrapped round the *book block* and glued to the spine: the usual way of attaching a paperback cover.
drop	See *chapter drop*.
dtp	*desktop publishing*. Dtp software is used by book designers to design and output the pages of books. Together with *photo-editing* software, it places most of the functions of the *compositor* in the hands of the *designer*.

dustjacket (jacket)	paper outer cover, with the title of the book printed on it, wrapped around the case of a case-bound book (occasionally, around the cover of a paperback book), traditionally to protect it from dust — today, also advertising the book. See *cover*.
em	the width of a capital letter M, always taken to be the same as the *point size* of the type in question (so an em of 10-point Times is 10 points) and used as a measurement of width, particularly as applied to *indents*, *spaces*, and *dashes*.
en	the width of a *lower-case* n, always taken to be half the *point size* of the type in question (so an en of 10-point Univers is 5 points) and used as a measurement of width, particularly of *spaces* and *dashes*. The *arabic figures* of most fonts are also one en wide.
endmatter	collective term for the parts of a book which come after the last chapter (e.g. notes, appendices, index).
endpaper	a folded sheet of paper, often of a different material from the pages, which attaches the outer pages of the *sewn middle* to the boards of a *case*d book. *To endpaper*: to attach endpapers.
EPS	*encapsulated PostScript*, one of two image-file formats generally accepted by *dtp* software and *imagesetters*. The other is *TIFF*.
filmsetting	*typesetting* by producing an image of type on film or bromide paper. Originally, the image was projected through a negative master using a simple light source — more recently electronically stored characters were exposed to film by means of cathode ray tubes or lasers. Filmsetters have been eclipsed by *imagesetters*.
finial	short finishing stroke of a letter-form, the point at which a calligrapher's pen would leave the paper.
foldout (folding leaf)	an outsized leaf which is folded to fit within the page size of the book. Sometimes *tipped on* to an adjacent page; sometimes bound in as an extension of a normal page of the book.
folio	(1) printed page number in a book; (2) the size of a standard sheet of printing paper folded in half. See *quarto*, *octavo*.
font	single alphabet of capitals and *lower-case* letters, usually equipped with figures, punctuation, and some special characters, such as fi and fl ligatures, which represents one part of a *typeface* or family of typefaces. E.g. Helvetica Bold Condensed, which is part of the Helvetica family of typefaces.
foot margin	see *margins*.
foredge	the outer edge of a page, which is trimmed when the book is bound.
fore margin	see *margins*.
French-sewn	see *sewing*.
frontispiece	illustration, or other formal page which faces the *title page*. Traditionally a leaf of *art paper tipped on* to the *half-title verso*: today, more frequently printed on the half-title verso itself.
gather	in book-binding, place *sections* in the right order, ready for *sewing* or *perfect binding*.

gloss art paper	paper to which an extrememly smooth coating has been applied, making it suitable for the most demanding *halftone* and colour printing. See *art paper*, *matt art paper*, *satin*.
grain direction	the direction in which the fibres of paper lie. Paper stretches more readily in the direction of the grain and folds more easily parallel to it. Paper sizes are expressed with the grain direction last (so 450 x 640 mm implies long grain, the grain running along the long edge of the sheet), but page sizes are not. See *page sizes*.
grid	designer's plan for the structure of a page, giving guidance for the positioning of text and pictures. See *layout*.
gsm	*grams per square metre*. The standard measurement of the weight of paper.
gutter	the inner edge of the *back*, or *inner margin*, where the page curves and recedes into darkness.
half-title	Traditionally, the first printed page of a book, giving the title. Half-title pages once functioned as dust-covers before the book was bound. Today, they save the title page from being partly obscured and rendered incapable of opening flat by attachment to the *endpaper*.
halftone	the most common way of rendering tone when printing. The image is divided into a regular pattern of dots which vary in size according to the darkness of the image at that point. Most book printers use half-tone screens of between 150 and 200 *lines per inch*. See *line image*.
hardback	see *case binding*.
house style	set of rules and guidelines devised to produce uniformity of editorial treatment of text and/or visual presentation.
imagesetter	computerized device for inscribing text and images onto film using an electronically controlled laser beam. Essentially similar to laser *film-setters*, imagesetters differ in having sufficient memory and processor power to handle images at high speed and to output imposed film. Unlike some filmsetters, imagesetters work from *PostScript* files. See *imposition*, *platesetter*.
imposition	laying out pages for printing in such a way that, when the printed sheet is folded, the pages fall in the correct order.
indent	align type at a distance from the left or right of the text *measure*. See *em*, *en*, *point*.
inner margin	see *margins*.
inset	place one folded sheet inside another to make a *section*.
ISBN	*international standard book number*. The identifying code used by book-ordering systems — issued, for a fee, by the ISBN Agency (UK address: Woolmead House West, Bear Lane, Farnham, Surrey, GU9 7LG).
italic	sloping type, calligraphic in origin, originally conceived as an alternative to *roman* (upright) type, subsequently used in combination with roman type to imply emphasis, or to distinguish foreign words and the titles of published works. Italic may also be used as display type or to identify a letter or word under discussion. *This is italic.*

jacket	see *dustjacket*.
justify	justified text is set to the full *measure*, with variable word-spacing, so that it produces a straight vertical margin at both sides. *Unjustified*, also called *ragged*, text has an uneven right-hand edge and fixed word spacing. *Dtp* software uses the term 'justification' to cover the whole question of how the text should be aligned (*centred*, justified, or unjustified) and whether or not it should be expanded with variable interlinear spacing (*leading*) to fill a fixed depth.
kerning	traditionally, filing or cutting the body of metal type to reduce space between letters. Today, to remove or add space between individual letters. Because most *PostScript* fonts are designed to work at text sizes (9 pt to 14 pt), they need kerning when used in large display sizes. See *tracking*.
laid paper	traditionally, paper which bore the impression of the wire mesh on which it was dried. Today, a similar effect is produced by embossing paper after it has been made.
landscape	of pages or images, having greater width than height. See *page sizes*.
layout	either a *grid* or the grid with elements of text and illustration positioned within it. See *grid*.
leader dots	horizontal lines of dots which connect items in one column with items in another. Encountered on contents pages, inventories, price lists, etc.
leading	so-called because *compositors* of metal type used strips of lead alloy to increase the space between lines of type, leading is usually expressed in *points* and prescribes the distance between the *baselines* of one line of type and the next.
letterpress	printing process whereby paper is pressed onto the inked surface of metal type and engraved blocks. The prevalent printing technology from the fifteenth century to the middle of the twentieth.
line image	an image which contains only solid areas (i.e. no variety of tone). An ink drawing is usually a line image even when tone is implied by means of hatching. A pencil drawing is not a line image because the mark of the pencil contains a variety of shades of grey. See *half-tone*.
lining figures	figures of the height of capital letters (*cap height*). Appropriately used with capital display lines, Times, and most sans-serif faces. These are lining figures: 1234567890. See *old-style figures*.
lithography (*offset lithography, litho*)	printing process which depends upon the mutual repulsion of grease and water. A grease-receptive image holds ink whilst the rest of the printing surface holds water. Originally, the printing surface was a stone and the paper was pressed directly onto its surface. The invention of *offset* lithography — where the stone is replaced by a pitted metal plate and the image is first printed onto a rubber-coated cylinder and thence transferred (or offset) to the paper — enabled lithography by the 1960's to overtake letterpress as the dominant printing technology.
lower case	letters which are neither capitals nor *small caps*, so-called because of their position in the cases of type used by hand *compositors*.

l.p.i.	*lines per inch*, the measure of *resolution* of a *half-tone* image.
making	a batch of one size and type of paper made at a paper mill. Paper ordered in a making quantity is usually cheaper per sheet than the same paper bought 'off the shelf'.
margins	the empty spaces around the text or illustration area of a page. In traditional order of size: *back*, or *inner margin*; *top margin*; *fore*, or *outer margin*; *foot margin*. See *gutter*, *foredge*.
masking	see *cropping*.
matt art paper	paper to which a non-shiny coating has been applied, making it suitable for most halftone and colour printing without having the reflective sheen of a gloss art paper. See *coated cartridge* and *gloss art paper*.
measure (text measure)	the width of the text area or column, usually given in *ems* of the type size, *picas*, or millimetres.
mould-made paper	paper which has been produced by a semi-mechanized craft process which gives it a rough absorbent surface without the lines of *laid paper*.
octavo	the page size resulting from folding a standard paper size into eighths (e.g. *demy octavo*).
OCR	*optical-character-recognition* software converts a scanned image of a page of type, or typing, into a text file capable of being edited.
offset lithography	see *lithography*.
old-style figures	figures based on the *x-height* of the *lower-case* alphabet. They are the traditional and most natural partners of most *seriffed* typefaces (but not of Times). These are old-style figures: 0123456789. See *lining figures*.
optical centring	the optical centre of a page, or of a space within a page is somewhat higher than its true geometric centre. The precise position of the optical centre is a matter of subjective judgement. Nevertheless, it features frequently in designers' instructions to printers.
orphan (club line)	the first line of a paragraph separated from the rest of the paragraph by a page-break. To be avoided. See *widow*.
outer margin	see *margins*.
outturn sheet	(1) sample sheet of a *making* of paper provided by the mill for approval prior to delivery; (2) sample printed sheets supplied by the printer for approval before binding.
Ozalid	chemically-based proofing system which produces rough monochrome proofs from film, useful for checking text or that the right items are on the right pages. Not suitable for checking quality.
page sizes	pages which are taller than they are wide are called *portrait* pages. Those which are wider than they are tall are *landscape*. Page sizes should be given with the height before the width (so, 210 x 297 mm is a landscape page, and 246 x 189 mm is a portrait page).
Pantone	colour-matching system which allocates number codes to colours, giving designers and printers a common form of reference.
paperback	book with a flexible board cover. See *perfect binding*.

PDF	portable document format, used by Adobe Acrobat. PostScript files can be converted into PDF files for Internet display, or for processing by *imposition* software. Also ideal for presenting documents in CD-Rom form.
perfect binding	method of *paperback* book-binding wherein the folded *sections* are gathered, their backs cut off, and the back of the resulting pages glued directly to the inside of the cover. Economic for long runs, but not to be preferred to *sewn binding* for strength or ease of use.
perfector	printing machine capable of printing both sides of a sheet of paper in one pass through the machine.
pH	value which signifies the acidity or alkalinity of a substance: pH7 is neutral; above pH7 is alkaline; below pH7 is acid.
photo-editing software	software which enables the designer to size, crop, and retouch illustrations ready for manipulation by dtp software.
Pica	(1) the standard of type measurement used in the UK and the USA; (2) [without the initial capital] a 12-point *em* of that standard, used as a measurement of width and depth of text areas, spaces, and illustrations. See *Cicero*.
plate	(1) the metal, plastic, or stiff-paper sheet which carries the image in *lithography* and from which it is printed; (2) a single page of illustrations, printed separately from the text of a book, usually on different paper. Increasingly rare since litho printing facilitates incorporation of images into text.
platesetter	computerized device which inscribes text and images direct to special *litho plates*. Similar to an *imagesetter* but, because there is no opportunity to impose the pages by hand, *imposition* software must be used.
point	the point is the smallest unit of measurement of type. Equivalent to approximately $\frac{1}{72}$ of an inch, there is a small difference between a point in the Anglo-American *Pica* standard and the European *Cicero*, or *Didot*, standard. Points are used to describe the size of type, *leading*, interlinear space, and can optionally be used for text areas and the size of illustrations.
portrait	of pages or images, having height greater than width. See *page sizes*.
positional scan	low-resolution *scan* used at the design stage to show the position, size and *cropping* (or *masking*) of a picture. Positionals must be replaced with high-resolution scans before outputting as film.
PostScript	the industry-standard system for digitizing type. PostScript fonts appear to produce more even letter spacing than other systems such as Truetype. There are also PostScript page-description and image file formats. See *EPS*.
prelims	preliminary pages of a book, often numbered with *roman folios*, which traditionally include: *half-title*, half-title *verso*, *title page*, title verso, contents, and acknowledgements.
press	*printing machine*. (Also used to mean printing or publishing company.)

preview	in *dtp* and photo-editing sofware, low-resolution version of a scanned image used internally by the software to save memory, the full-resolution version being substituted on output.
printing	producing multiple copies of text or images on paper by mechanical or electronic means. In book printing, generally taken to mean *offset lithography* unless another process is specified.
quad	an *em* space. See *em*.
Quad Demy	see *Demy*.
Quad Royal	see *Royal*.
quarto	the page size resulting from folding a standard paper size into quarters (e.g. Crown Quarto).
RA1	paper size, 610 x 860 mm.
RA2	paper size, 430 x 610 mm.
ragged text	see *justify*.
recto	right-hand page.
resolution	a measure of the degree of fineness at which an image or text is originated, *scanned*, or output on an *imagesetter* or *platesetter* (*dots per inch*), or as a screened *half-tone* (*lines per inch*). High-resolution images are needed for printing. Lower-resolution images may be used for design and layout purposes. See *preview*.
reverse out	cause (usually type) to appear white against a comparatively dark background.
roman	the basic form of any family of fonts. Upright — as opposed to *italic*, which slopes — and of medium weight — as compared with *bold*, which is heavy. This is roman.
roman numerals	I, II, III, IV, etc., as opposed to *arabic figures* (1, 2, 3, 4, etc.).
Royal (Metric Royal)	paper size, 480 x 635 mm. Quad Royal is 960 x 1270 mm.
rtf	*rich-text format*. A text file format which preserves important formatting (e.g. italics) and is accepted by most *dtp* and *word-processing* software on both Macs and PCs.
running head	line of type, usually at the head of the page, repeated on every page of a book, chapter, or subsection: typically giving the title of the book, chapter, or subsection.
saddle-stitching	see *wire-stitching*.
sans serif	without *serifs*. Gill Sans, Univers, and Helvetica are examples of sans serif typefaces. This is Gill Sans Light.
satin	of paper, a form of *art paper* the surface of which is smoother than *matt art* but less shiny than *gloss art*. The term *silk* is used for similar papers.
scan	see *scanner*.
scanner	device which produces electronic image files (*scans*) from photographs, artwork, or transparencies.

search-and-replace	feature of *word-processing* and *dtp* software which finds an item of text or formatting and replaces it with another. Use search-and-replace, for instance, to eliminate double spaces and replace *lining* with *old-style figures*.
section (signature)	in book-binding, a section is a folded sheet, or a number of folded sheets inset into each other, which forms one of several units to be *gathered* before *sewing* or *perfect binding*.
serif	short horizontal or slanted line at the terminal of *ascender*, *descender*, or *finial*.
set-off	the accidental transfer of ink from one sheet of paper to the next in a stack or bound book.
sewing (sewn, French-sewn binding)	holding the pages of a *section* together and the sections of a book to one-another using thread. See *perfect binding*, *wire stitching*.
sheet-fed press	a sheet-fed printing *press* prints onto sheets of paper of the size necessary to produce the correct page size when folded and trimmed. See *web*.
show-through	the appearance through a page of printing which is on the other side or on an adjacent page. If marked, a sign of inadequate opacity.
side-stabbing (stabbing)	see *wire-stitching*.
signature	see *section*.
signature mark	a signature mark is a small black rectangle printed onto the outside of the back of a *section* (thus invisible when bound) which enables the binder to see that he or she has all the sections in the right order.
silk	see *satin*.
sizing	of pictures, indicating the required reduction or enlargement (usually expressed as a percentage of the original size) or carrying out these processes. See *S/S*.
small caps	capital letters of the height and weight of *lower-case* letters. They are used on their own, or in combination with capitals, in *display* setting (subheads, *running heads*) and, sometimes, to highlight the first phrase of a chapter or subsection. Small caps may also be used for some capitalized initials which occur in the middle of text (e.g. A.D., B.C.), post codes, and professional qualifications like B.A., D.PHIL, F.S.A.
spaces	horizontal spaces may be variable (as in the inter-word spacing of *justified* text) or fixed (as in the inter-word spacing of *unjustified* type). In either case, *dtp* software allows the user to set parameters. For *indenting* and separating words, the traditional compositor had a variety of fixed spaces at his disposal. Dtp users can either use the *en*-space key to make *ens* and *ems* (1 *em* = 2 x 1 *en*) or substitute manual *kerning* for the smaller fixed spaces. Vertical spaces are traditionally measured in *points*. Decimals of a millimetre provide an alternative if your grid has been worked out in millimetres.
SRA1	paper size, 640 x 900 mm.
SRA2	paper size, 450 x 640 mm.

S/S	*same size*, referring to pictures, meaning 'requiring no reduction or enlargement'. See *sizing*.
stabbing	see *sidestabbing*.
supercalender	see *calender*.
superior figures	*arabic* figures of reduced size which are raised approximately to align at the top with *ascenders* and capitals, used for footnote references. See *superscript characters*.
superscript characters	characters of reduced size which are raised above the height of normal characters and may be positioned above them or alongside them; used, for example, in mathematical setting. See *superior figures*.
text measure	see *measure*.
TIFF	*tagged-image file format*, one of two image-file formats generally accepted by *dtp* software and *imagesetters*. The other is *EPS*.
tinted paper	paper coloured throughout instead of merely on the surface.
tip-in	see *tip-on*.
tip-on (tip-in)	a leaf or small section which is pasted along its back edge to a page of the book. To tip on (or in) is to attach such a leaf. See *fold-out*.
title page	The page which gives the title, author, publisher, and place and date of publication of the book. Traditionally, the third page of the *prelims*. See *half-title*.
tolerance	(1) the maximum distance by which a fold or *trim* may be expected to vary from its correct position — usually 3 mm; (2) the maximum amount by which the supply of paper or printed items is permitted by contract to vary from the ordered quantity — usually 5%.
tracking	enlarging or reducing the space between letters for a selected body of text (as compared with *kerning*, which is applied individually to pairs of letters). Large sizes of *lower-case* type may need negative tracking (less space), whilst lines of capitals or *small caps* require positive tracking. If you wish to give PostScript type the appearance and legibility of metal type you may have to track it a little.
trim	the margin of paper cut from the edges of a folded book (or other printed item) to produce the finished product.
typeface	either a *font*, such as Times italic, or a family of fonts, e.g. Times.
typescale	ruler for measuring type, particularly horizontally. Usually featuring two or three popular type sizes and millimetres. If metal, also a useful cutting edge. See *depthscale*.
typesetting	preparing text for printing by presenting it in type, whether metal, film, or digital. See *filmsetting*, *imagesetter*.
typographer	designer skilled in the arrangement of type. A typographer need not be a book designer, but a book designer should be a typographer. See *book designer*, *compositor*.
unjustified text	see *justify*.
verso	left-hand page.
web press	web presses print onto reels of paper which are then sheeted (cut into sheets of the required size for binding). See *sheet-fed*.

widow	the last line of a paragraph, appearing at the top of a page. Never to be permitted in professional typesetting. See *orphan*.
wire-stitching (saddle stitching)	method of binding single-section books or booklets by securing the pages with two or more staples through the spine. Depending on the weight of the paper, it is inadvisable to attempt to bind a book of more than 48 or 64 pages in this way. Bookbinders always mean wire, rather than thread, when they speak of stitching. Another method of stitching, *side-stabbing*, which is not normally used for bookbinding, involves stitching through the whole thickness of the book close to the back edge of the pages.
word-processing	word-processing software (e.g. Word or WordPerfect) has become almost sophisticated enough to rival *dtp* software in the preparation of illustrated documents. However, whilst it is indispensable for editing text ready for dtp software, it still does not offer the flexibility and image handling power required by the designer.
wove (book-wove)	rough, uncoated paper of relatively high bulk and opacity used for unillustrated books. May be off-white or cream.
x-height	the height of those *lower-case* letters which do not have *ascenders*; specifically, the height of the letter x.

index

THE NUMBERS after each entry are chapter and section numbers. In most cases the indexed item is found on the same page as the start of the section: in a few larger sections it may be necessary turn one or two pages to find it.

abbreviations, list of 3.12
acknowledgements 3.11
adhesive 8.6.7
aesthetics (v. economics) 4.5
appendix 3.15
ascender 7.3
asymmetry 5.6
author-date system of references
    3.16.1
author's
    corrections 8.7.3
    preface 3.10

bibliography 3.17
binding 1.5
    automation 1.5.9
    case 1.5.7, 2.2.6
    materials 2.4.1
    paperback 1.5.6, 1.5.8
    perfect 1.5.6
bleed 4.3, 5.7
blocking 1.5.7
    blind 1.5.7
blurb 7.17.2
board 2.2.6
    grey 2.2.6
    mill 2.2.6
book
    block 1.5.4, 1.5.6
    parts of 3

calliper (thickness) of paper 2.3.4
capitals (and lower-case) 7.5
caption 6.8.2
case (cased) binding 1.5.7
CD-R (recordable compact disk)
    8.4.1, 8.4.3
classification of typefaces 7.6
centring
    on measure 7.12
    optical 7.16.3
coated
    cartridge 2.2.1
    papers 2.2.1
collating (gathering) 1.5.3

colour
    on covers and dustjackets
        7.17.2
    output 1.3.2
    paper 2.3.7
    printing 1.4.1
    spot 1.4.2
column 5.5
    break 7.14
computer-to-plate (ctp) 1.3.1
contents list 3.7, 7.16.3
cover
    design 7.17
    drawn-on 1.5.8
Cromalin 8.7.5
cropping 6.6
ctp (computer-to-plate) 1.3.1

dashes 7.15.2
dedication 3.6
densitometer 1.4.1
depth scale 8.6.2
descender 7.3
design
    agreeing 8.7.1
    without a computer 8.5
    book 8.7.2
desktop publishing 8.4
display 7.16
double-page spread 5.3
dpi dots-per-inch 6.9.1, 6.9.2
dustjacket 7.17

editorial style 9
en
    space 7.15.1
    dash 7.15.2
endmatter 3.14, 3.15–3.18
endpaper 1.5.5
EPS (Encapsulated PostScript) 6.4
equipment 8

face 7.2
film 6.9.3, 8.7.4
    checking 8.7.5

folding 1.5.2
folio 3.19
font (fount) 7.1, 7.2
foreword 3.9
format 4, 4.8
    and economy 4.2
    grid 4.8
four-colour printing 1.4.1
frontispiece 3.3

gathering (collating) 1.5.3, 1.5.6
grain 2.2.4, 2.3.2, 4.6
greyscale 6.9.1
grid 4.8, 5.2, 5.5
    placing of elements 5.8
    samples 5.5
gsm (grams per square metre)
    2.2.6, 2.3.1, 7.17.1
gutter 5.3

half-title 3.1, 3.2, 7.16.2
halftone image 6.3, 6.4
hardware 8.2, 8.4.1
Harvard system of references
    3.16.1
hyphen 7.15.2
hyphenation 7.13

illustrated books 6.8.2
illustration 6
image 6
    colour, outputting 6.9.1
    cut-out 6.8.1
    file format 6.4
    masking (cropping) 6.6
    outputting 6.9
    positional 6.2, 6.5
    sizing 6.5
    types of 6.3
imagesetter 1.3
imposition 1.5.1
index 3.18
ink 1.4
instruments 8.6
introduction 3.13
ISBN 3.5

jacket 7.17
justification 4.8, 7.12

kerning 7.11

laid paper 2.2.4
landscape (portrait or) 4.7
layout 5
legibility 7.10.3
letterpress 1.1
lightbox 8.6.9
line image 6.3, 6.4
lining figures 7.5.2, 8.7.2
list
    of abbreviations 3.12
    contents 3.7
    of illustrations 3.8
lithography, offset 1.1
lower-case (and capitals) 7.5
lpi (lines-per-inch) 6.9.1

Mac 8.2, 8.4.1
machine, printing 1.4, 1.4.2, 1.4.3, 1.4.4
margins 5.1, 5.5
marking artwork 6.7
masking (cropping) 6.6
matt art paper 2.2.1
measure 5.1, 7.12
measurement, units of 5.4

notes 3.16

ocr (optical character recognition) 8.7.2
old-style figures 7.5.2, 8.7.2
opacity (of paper) 2.3.3
optical centring 7.16.3
orphan line 7.14
output 8.7.4
outturn sheet 8.7.5
Ozalid 8.7.5

page
    break 7.14
    numbering 3.19
    size 4.4, 4.7, 4.8
    title 3.4
Pantone 1.4.2
paper 2.2
    acidity 2.3.5
    art 2.2.1
    bulk 2.3.1
    calender 2.3.4
    cartridge 2.2.2
    coated 2.2.1
    grain 2.2.4, 2.3.2, 4.6
    making quantity 2.2.3, 2.3.1
    offset 2.2.2
    opacity 2.3.1, 2.3.3
    plastic 2.4.2

size 4.4, 4.7, 4.8
smoothness 2.3.6
speciality 2.2.5
surface 2.3.6
thickness (caliper) 2.3.4
tint (shade) 2.3.7
weight 2.3.1
wove 2.2.3
paperback 1.5.6, 1.5.8
PC 8.2, 8.4.1
pen 8.6.5
pencil 8.6.6
perfect binding 1.5.6
perfector 1.4.3
peripherals 8.4.3
pica 5.4, 7.11
picture (image) 6
    book 6.8.1
    cut-out 6.8.1
plate, printing 1.4
platesetter 1.3.1
point (measure) 5.4, 7.11
portrait or landscape 4.7
positional scan 1.2, 6.2
PostScript 7.10.1
preface 3.10
prelimimnary pages (prelims) 7.16.3
printer (peripheral) 8.4.3
printing 1.4
    colour 1.4.1
    machine 1.4
    perfecting 1.4.3
    plate 1.4
    web 1.4.4
procedure 8.7
proofing 8.7.3

ragged (justification) 7.12
range (left/right) 7.12
recto 3.4, 5.6
references 3.16
resolution 6.9.1

sans serif 7.4, 7.8
satin (silk) art paper 2.2.1
scalpel 8.6.4
scanner 8.4.3
scanning 1.2, 6.2, 6.4, 6.9.1
self-ends 1.5.5
serif 7.4, 7.7
sewing 1.5.4
sewn middle 1.5.4
size
    ISO 4.4
    page 4.2, 4.4, 4.7, 4.8
    paper 4.2, 4.4, 4.7, 4.8
    standard 4.4
    type 7.11, 7.16.1
small capitals 7.5.1
software

desktop-publishing 8.4.2
    photo-editing 8.4.2
    word-processor 8.3
spaces 7.15.1
spacing
    vertical (of display type) 7.16.1
specimen page 8.7.1
spine 7.12.2
spread, double-page 5.3
stitching (wire) 1.5.4
style, editorial 9
subheadings 7.16.2
superior figures 3.16
symmetry 5.6

text 3.14
TIFF (Tagged-Image File Format) 6.4
tipping in (on) 1.5.3, 7.16.3
title
    page 3.4, 7.16.3
    verso 3.5, 7.16.3
tracking 7.11
trim 4.3, 5.7
TrueType 7.10.1
type 7
    classification 7.6
    display 7.16
    faces 7.2, 7.10
        choosing 7.10
        described 7.10.2
        which to use 7.10.3
        legibility 7.10.3
        appearance 7.10.3
        economy 7.10.3
    justification 7.12
    leading 7.11
    metal 1.1
    sans serif 7.4, 7.8
    serif 7.4, 7.7
    size 7.11, 7.16.1
    spacing 7.11, 7.15.1
typescale 5.4, 8.6.1
typography 7, 7.9

units of measurement 5.4
unjustified setting 4.8, 5.5, 7.12
upper-case (capitals) 7.5

verso 3.2, 5.6
    title 3.5

web offset 1.4.4
weight(of paper/board) 2.3.1
widow line 7.14
word break (split) 7.13
word processor 8.3
wove (paper) 2.2.3

x-height 7.10.3, 7.11